English as a Second Language

Secondary Cycle Two
Year Three

Literature *Plus*
Reading for Pleasure

GRAFICOR
CHENELIÈRE ÉDUCATION

Quest
English as a Second Language
Secondary Cycle Two, Year Three

Literature *Plus*

Activities: Gillian Baxter

© 2010 Chenelière Education Inc.

Editor: Susan Roy
Project manager: Lee Ann Balazuc
Proofreader: My-Trang Nguyen
Copyright researcher: Karine Perron
Photo researcher: Rachel Irwin
Cover designer: Karina Dupuis
Book designer and typesetter: Fenêtre sur cour
Printer: Imprimeries Transcontinental

GRAFICOR

CHENELIÈRE ÉDUCATION

7001 Saint-Laurent Blvd.
Montréal (Québec) Canada H2S 3E3
Telephone: 514 273-1066
Fax: 450 461-3834 / 1 888 460-3834
info@cheneliere.ca

ISBN 978-2-7652-1282-9

Dépôt légal : 1er trimestre 2010
Bibliothèque et Archives nationales du Québec
Bibliothèque et Archives Canada

Printed in Canada

2   3   4   5   6   ITG   14   13   12   11   10

We acknowledge the financial support of the
Government of Canada through the Book
Publishing Industry Development Program
(BPIDP) for our publishing activities.

Government of Quebec – Tax credit for book
publishing – Administered by SODEC.

Member of the CERC

Member of the
Association nationale
des éditeurs de livres

ASSOCIATION
NATIONALE
DES ÉDITEURS
DE LIVRES

Table of Contents

Note: All texts are original and therefore may contain Canadian, American or British English spelling.

Tobias Wolff was born in Birmingham, Alabama in 1945, and is best known for his detailed and sensitive short stories and memoirs. He graduated from Oxford University in England with an Honours degree in English Literature. An award-winning writer, Wolff has published several collections of short stories and two novels, as well as dozens of magazine pieces.

Before Reading

1. Choose the word on each line that does not mean the same thing as the others.

a) fret	bother	worry	comfort
b) whirl	spin	rotate	stay
c) mope	pout	sulk	rejoice
d) wheedle	influence	accept	persuade
e) plead	ask	beg	answer

2. Read the title of the story. What do you think it will be about?

3. In what ways do you think parents should be role models for their children?

While Reading

4. Pay attention to descriptions of the main characters in the story. While you read, write down information about the characters' personality traits, their strengths and weaknesses, how they act, what they think, what they say and what they do. Write your ideas in a graphic organizer.

5. Make a list of words or groups of words that describe the setting of the story.

6. List ten new words you learned while reading. Provide a definition for each one and write a sentence to show its meaning.

Powder

by Tobias Wolff

Just before Christmas my father took me skiing at Mount Baker. He'd had to fight for the privilege of my company, because my mother was still angry with him for sneaking me into a nightclub during our last visit, to see Thelonius
5 Monk.

He wouldn't give up. He promised, hand on heart, to take good care of me and have me home for dinner on Christmas Eve, and she relented. But as we were checking out of the lodge that morning it began to snow, and in this
10 snow he observed some rare quality that made it necessary for us to get in one last run. We got in several last runs. He was indifferent to my fretting. Snow whirled around us in bitter, blinding squalls, hissing like sand, and still we skied. As the lift bore us to the peak yet again, my father looked at
15 his watch and said, "Criminy. This'll have to be a fast one."

By now I couldn't see the trail. There was no point in trying. I stuck to him like white on rice and did what he did and somehow made it to the bottom without sailing off a cliff. We returned our skis and my father put chains on the
20 Austin-Healey while I swayed from foot to foot, clapping

my mittens and wishing I were home. I could see everything. The green tablecloth, the plates with the holly pattern, the red candles waiting to be lit.

We passed a diner on our way out. "You want some
25 soup?" my father asked. I shook my head. "Buck up," he said. "I'll get you there. Right, doctor?"

I was supposed to say, "Right, doctor," but I didn't say anything.

A state trooper waved us down outside the resort. A pair
30 of **sawhorses** were blocking the road. The trooper came up to our car and bent down to my father's window. His face was **bleached** by the cold. Snowflakes clung to his eyebrows and to the fur trim of his jacket and cap.

"Don't tell me," my father said.

35 The trooper told him. The road was closed. It might get cleared, it might not. Storm took everyone by surprise. So much, so fast. Hard to get people moving. Christmas Eve. What can you do?

My father said, "Look. We're talking about four, five
40 inches. I've taken this car through worse than that."

The trooper straightened up, boots creaking. His face was out of sight but I could hear him. "The road is closed."

My father sat with both hands on the wheel, rubbing the wood with his thumbs. He looked at the barricade for a
45 long time. He seemed to be trying to master the idea of it. Then he thanked the trooper, and with a weird, old-maidy show of caution turned the car around. "Your mother will never forgive me for this," he said.

"We should have left before," I said. "Doctor."

50 He didn't speak to me again until we were both in a booth at the diner, waiting for our burgers. "She won't forgive me," he said. "Do you understand? Never."

"I guess," I said, but no **guesswork** was required; she wouldn't forgive him.

55 "I can't let that happen." He bent toward me. "I'll tell you what I want. I want us to be together again. Is that what you want?"

I wasn't sure, but I said, "Yes, sir."

He bumped my chin with his knuckles. "That's all I
60 needed to hear."

When we finished eating he went to the pay phone in the back of the diner, then joined me in the booth again. I figured he'd called my mother, but he didn't give a report. He sipped at his coffee and stared out the window at the
65 empty road. "Come on, come on," he said, though not to me. A little while later he said it again. When the trooper's car went past, lights flashing, he got up and dropped some money on the check. "Okay. Vámonos."

The wind had died. The snow was falling straight
70 down, less of it now and lighter. We drove away from the resort, right up to the barricade. "Move it," my father told me. When I looked at him he said, "What are you waiting for?" I got out and dragged one of the sawhorses aside, then pushed
75 it back after he drove through. When I got inside the car he said, "Now you're an accomplice. We go down together." He put the car in gear and gave me a look.
80 "Joke, son."

VOCABULARY

bleached: made white

guesswork: making guesses

sawhorse: a frame used to support wood

Down the first long stretch I watched the road behind us, to see if the trooper was on our tail. The barricade vanished. Then there was nothing but snow: snow on the road, snow kicking up from the chains, snow on the trees, snow in the sky; and our trail in the snow. Then I faced forward and had a shock. The lay of the road behind us had been marked by our own tracks, but there were no tracks ahead of us. My father was breaking virgin snow between a line of tall trees. He was humming "Stars Fell on Alabama." I felt snow brush along the floorboards under my feet. To keep my hands from shaking I clamped them between my knees.

My father grunted in a thoughtful way and said, "Don't ever try this yourself."

"I won't."

"That's what you say now, but someday you'll get your license and then you'll think you can do anything. Only you won't be able to do this. You need, I don't know—a certain instinct."

"Maybe I have it."

"You don't. You have your strong points, but not this. I only mention it because I don't want you to get the idea this is something just anybody can do. I'm a great driver.

Tobias Wolff

That's not a virtue, okay? It's just a fact, and one you should be aware of. Of course you have to give the old heap some
105 credit, too. There aren't many cars I'd try this with. Listen!"

I listened. I heard the slap of the chains, the stiff, jerky **rasp** of the wipers, the purr of the engine. It really did purr. The old heap was almost new. My father couldn't afford it, and kept promising to sell it, but here it was.

110 I said, "Where do you think that policeman went to?"

"Are you warm enough?" He reached over and cranked up the blower. Then he turned off the wipers. We didn't need them. The clouds had brightened. A few sparse, feathery flakes drifted into our slipstream and were swept
115 away. We left the trees and entered a broad field of snow that ran level for a while and then tilted sharply downward. Orange stakes had been planted at intervals in two parallel lines and my father ran a course between them, though they were far enough apart to leave considerable
120 doubt in my mind as to where exactly the road lay. He was humming again, doing little scat riffs around the melody.

"Okay then. What are my strong points?"

"Don't get me started," he said. "It'd take all day."

"Oh, right. Name one."

125 "Easy. You always think ahead."

True. I always thought ahead. I was a boy who kept his clothes on numbered hangers to ensure proper rotation. I bothered my teachers for homework assignments far ahead of their due dates so I could make up schedules. I thought
130 ahead, and that was why I knew that there would be other troopers waiting for us at the end of our ride, if we even got there. What I did not know was that my father would wheedle and plead his way past them—he didn't sing "O Tannenbaum" but just about—and get me home for dinner,
135 buying a little more time before my mother decided to make the split final. I knew we'd get caught; I was resigned to it. And maybe for this reason I stopped moping and began to enjoy myself.

Why not? This was one for
140 the books. Like being in a speedboat, only better. You can't go down hill in a boat. And it

was all ours. And it kept coming, the **laden** trees, the
unbroken surface of snow, the sudden white vistas. Here
145 and there I saw hints of the road, ditches, fences, stakes,
but not so many that I could have found my way. But then
I didn't have to. My father in his forty-eighth year,
rumpled, kind, **bankrupt of** honour, flushed with
certainty. He was a great driver. All persuasion, no coercion.
150 Such subtlety at the wheel, such tactful pedalwork. I
actually trusted him. And the best was yet to come—
switchbacks and **hairpins** impossible to describe.
Except maybe to say this: If you haven't driven fresh
powder, you haven't driven.

VOCABULARY

bankrupt of: without

hairpin: a sharp curve
in the road

laden: loaded down

switchback: a trail
that follows a zigzag
course

After Reading

1. Why was the boy's mother angry with his father?

2. When the snow started on Christmas Eve morning, what did the father decide to do?

3. How did the boy manage to make it to the bottom of the ski trail?

4. When they are in the diner, whom does the father call?

5. What do you learn about the boy's mother from the information provided in the text?

6. Using the notes you took about the father and son, create a Venn diagram to compare and contrast the two characters.

7. Describe the relationships between the different characters in the story. Provide information about a) the man and his son; b) the man and the boy's mother; c) the boy and his mother. Find information from the text to support your answers.

8. How do the father's driving abilities reflect how he approaches life in general? Find examples in the text to support your answer.

9. At what moment in the story does the boy's attitude towards the experience change? Why?

10. What do you think the boy means when he says, "If you haven't driven fresh powder, you haven't driven."

Beyond the Lines

11. Describe an experience you or someone you know had because of a snow storm or severe weather conditions.

12. Parents are expected to be role models for their children. Look at your answer to Question 3 in the Before Reading section. In what ways does the boy's father in this story go against traditional parenting roles? In what ways does he respect them?

13. The American poet Ralph Waldo Emerson said, "Do not go where the path may lead, go instead where there is no path and leave a trail." What do you think he meant? How is this reflected in the story "Powder"?

Anton Pavlovich Chekhov (1860–1904) was a Russian short-story writer, playwright and physician. He is considered to be one of the greatest writers in world literature, and his plays continue to be performed in modern theatres. Chekhov grew up in poverty, and became the sole supporter of his family at a very young age, writing humorous sketches and plays to make money. He wrote 13 plays and countless short stories during his relatively short lifetime. His work is known for its honest portrayal of human emotions through humorous dialogue.

Before Reading

1. Read the list of adjectives. Find and write the definition of each word.

dear	gloomy	poetical	sweet
detestable	gracious	repulsive	terrible
downcast	hateful	satisfied	thrilling
dreary	hollow	serene	wretched
enchanted	panicstricken	stingy	

2. Make a T-Chart and classify each of the words above as positive or negative.

3. Have you ever won a prize at a raffle or in another type of contest? What was it?

4. Do you know anyone who buys lottery tickets regularly? Has someone you know ever won the lottery?

While Reading

5. Find the adjectives listed in Question 1 in the text. Write down what or whom each word describes.

6. Pay attention to how the main characters change as the story progresses. Write down key words to track their development.

7. Plot the main events of the story on a pyramid of action. Include information about the five parts of the plot structure: Introduction, Rising Action, Climax, Falling Action, and Resolution.

The Lottery Ticket

by Anton Pavlovich Chekhov

I van Dmitritch, a middle-class man who lived with his family on an income of twelve hundred a year and was very well satisfied with his lot, sat down on the sofa after supper and began reading the newspaper.

5 "I forgot to look at the newspaper today," his wife said to him as she cleared the table. "Look and see whether the list of drawings is there."

"Yes, it is," said Ivan Dmitritch; "but hasn't your ticket lapsed?"

10 "No; I took the interest on Tuesday."

"What is the number?"

"Series 9,499, number 26."

"All right . . . we will look . . . 9,499 and 26."

Ivan Dmitritch had no faith in lottery luck, and would
15 not, as a rule, have consented to look at the lists of winning numbers, but now, as he had nothing else to do and as the newspaper was before his eyes, he passed his finger downwards along the column of numbers. And immediately, as though in mockery of his scepticism, no
20 further than the second line from the top, his eye was caught by the figure 9,499!

Unable to believe his eyes, he hurriedly dropped the paper on his knees without looking to see the number of the ticket, and, just as though some one had given him a douche of cold water, he felt an agreeable chill in the pit of the stomach; **tingling** and terrible and sweet!

"Masha, 9,499 is there!" he said in a hollow voice.

His wife looked at his astonished and panicstricken face, and realized that he was not joking.

"9,499?" she asked, turning pale and dropping the folded tablecloth on the table.

"Yes, yes . . . it really is there!"

"And the number of the ticket?"

"Oh yes! There's the number of the ticket too. But stay . . . wait! No, I say! Anyway, the number of our series is there! Anyway, you understand...."

Looking at his wife, Ivan Dmitritch gave a broad, senseless smile, like a baby when a bright object is shown it. His wife smiled too; it was as pleasant to her as to him that he only mentioned the series, and did not try to find out the number of the winning ticket. To torment and **tantalize** oneself with hopes of possible fortune is so sweet, so thrilling!

"It is our series," said Ivan Dmitritch, after a long silence. "So there is a probability that we have won. It's only a probability, but there it is!"

"Well, now look!"

"Wait a little. We have plenty of time to be disappointed. It's on the second line from the top, so the prize is seventy-five thousand. That's not money, but power, capital! And in a minute I shall look at the list, and there—26! Eh? I say, what if we really have won?"

The husband and wife began laughing and staring at one another in silence. The possibility of winning **bewildered** them; they could not have said, could not have dreamed, what they both needed that seventy-five thousand for, what they would buy, where they would go. They thought only of the figures 9,499 and 75,000 and pictured them in their imagination, while somehow they could not think of the happiness itself which was so possible.

Ivan Dmitritch, holding the paper in his hand, walked several times from corner to corner, and only when he had recovered from the first impression began dreaming a little.

65 "And if we have won," he said—"why, it will be a new life, it will be a transformation! The ticket is yours, but if it were mine I should, first of all, of course, spend twenty-five thousand on real property in the shape of an estate; ten thousand on immediate expenses, new furnishing . . .
70 travelling . . . paying debts, and so on . . . The other forty thousand I would put in the bank and get interest on it."

"Yes, an estate, that would be nice," said his wife, sitting down and dropping her hands in her lap.

"Somewhere in the Tula or Oryol provinces . . . In the
75 first place we shouldn't need a summer villa, and besides, it would always bring in an income."

And pictures came crowding on his imagination, each more gracious and poetical than the last. And in all these pictures he saw himself well-fed, serene, healthy, felt warm,
80 even hot! Here, after eating a summer soup, cold as ice, he lay on his back on the burning sand close to a stream or in the garden under a lime-tree . . . It is hot . . . His little boy and girl are crawling about near him, digging in the sand or catching ladybirds in the grass. He dozes sweetly,
85 thinking of nothing, and feeling all over that he need not go to the office today, tomorrow, or the day after. Or, tired of lying still, he goes to the hayfield, or to the forest for mushrooms, or watches the peasants catching fish with a net. When the sun sets he takes a towel and soap and
90 saunters to the bathing shed, where he undresses at his leisure, slowly rubs his bare chest with his hands, and goes into the water. And in the water, near the opaque soapy circles, little fish **flit** to and fro and
95 green water-weeds nod their heads. After bathing there is tea with cream and milk rolls. . . . In the evening a walk or *vint* with the neighbors. "Yes, it would be
100 nice to buy an estate," said his wife, also dreaming, and from

her face it was evident that she was enchanted by her thoughts.

105 Ivan Dmitritch pictured to himself autumn with its rains, its cold evenings, and its St. Martin's summer. At that season he would have 110 to take longer walks about the garden and beside the river, so as to get thoroughly chilled, and then drink a big glass of vodka and eat a salted mushroom or a **soused** 115 cucumber, and then—drink another . . . The children would come running from the kitchen-garden, bringing a carrot and a radish smelling of fresh earth . . .

And then, he would lie stretched full length on the sofa, and in leisurely fashion turn over the pages of some 120 illustrated magazine, or, covering his face with it and unbuttoning his waistcoat, give himself up to slumber. The St. Martin's summer is followed by cloudy, gloomy weather. It rains day and night, the bare trees weep, the wind is damp and cold. The dogs, the horses, the fowls—all are 125 wet, depressed, downcast. There is nowhere to walk; one can't go out for days together; one has to pace up and down the room, looking despondently at the grey window. It is **dreary**!

Ivan Dmitritch stopped and looked at his wife.

130 "I should go abroad, you know, Masha," he said.

And he began thinking how nice it would be in late autumn to go abroad somewhere to the South of France . . . to Italy . . . to India!

"I should certainly go abroad too," his wife said. "But 135 look at the number of the ticket!"

"Wait, wait! . . ."

He walked about the room and went on thinking. It occurred to him: what if his wife really did go abroad? It is pleasant to travel alone, or in the society of light, careless 140 women who live in the present, and not such as think and talk all the journey about nothing but their children, sigh,

and tremble with dismay over every **farthing**. Ivan Dmitritch imagined his wife in the train with a multitude of parcels, baskets, and bags; she would be sighing over
145 something, complaining that the train made her head ache, that she had spent so much money . . . At the stations he would continually be having to run for boiling water, bread and butter . . . She wouldn't have dinner because of its being too **dear** . . .

150 "She would **begrudge** me every farthing," he thought, with a glance at his wife. "The lottery ticket is hers, not mine! Besides, what is the use of her going abroad? What does she want there? She would shut herself up in the hotel, and not let me out of her sight . . . I know!"

155 And for the first time in his life his mind dwelt on the fact that his wife had grown elderly and plain, and that she was saturated through and through with the smell of cooking, while he was still young, fresh, and healthy, and might well have got married again.

160 "Of course, all that is silly nonsense," he thought; "but . . . why should she go abroad? What would she make of it? And yet she would go, of course . . . I can fancy . . . In reality it is all one to her, whether it is Naples or Klin. She would only be in my way. I should be dependent upon her.
165 I can fancy how, like a regular woman, she will lock the money up as soon as she gets it . . . She will look after her **relations** and grudge me every farthing."

Ivan Dmitritch thought of
170 her relations. All those wretched brothers and sisters and aunts and uncles would come crawling about as soon as they heard of the winning ticket, would begin
175 whining like beggars, and **fawning** upon them with oily, hypocritical smiles. Wretched, detestable people! If they were given anything, they would ask
180 for more; while if they were refused, they would swear at

VOCABULARY

begrudge: be reluctant to give

dear: expensive

dreary: dull

farthing: an old bronze coin (cent)

fawn: look for favour or attention by flattery

relations: family members

soused: pickled

them, **slander** them, and wish them every kind of misfortune.

Ivan Dmitritch remembered his own relations, and their faces, at which he had looked impartially in the past, struck him now as repulsive and hateful.

"They are such reptiles!" he thought.

And his wife's face, too, struck him as repulsive and hateful. Anger surged up in his heart against her, and he thought malignantly:

"She knows nothing about money, and so she is **stingy**. If she won it she would give me a hundred rubles, and put the rest away under lock and key."

And he looked at his wife, not with a smile now, but with **hatred**. She glanced at him too, and also with hatred and anger. She had her own daydreams, her own plans, her own reflections; she understood perfectly well what her husband's dreams were. She knew who would be the first to try to grab her winnings.

"It's very nice making daydreams at other people's expense!" is what her eyes expressed. "No, don't you dare!"

Her husband understood her look; hatred began stirring again in his breast, and in order to annoy his wife he glanced quickly, to spite her at the fourth page on the newspaper and read out triumphantly:

"Series 9,499, number 46! Not 26!"

Hatred and hope both disappeared at once, and it began immediately to seem to Ivan Dmitritch and his wife that their rooms were dark and small and low-pitched, that the supper they had been eating was not doing them good, but lying heavy on their stomachs, that the evenings were long and **wearisome**. . . .

"What the devil's the meaning of it?" said Ivan Dmitritch, beginning to be ill-humored. 'Wherever one steps there are bits of paper under one's feet, crumbs, husks. The rooms are never swept! One is simply forced to go out. Damnation take my soul entirely! I shall go and hang myself on the first aspen-tree!"

VOCABULARY

hatred: extreme dislike

slander: speak badly of

stingy: not generous

wearisome: boring

Anton Pavlovich Chekhov

After Reading

1. To whom does the lottery ticket belong?

2. How does Ivan Dmitritch feel about lotteries?

3. Why didn't Ivan check the number of the series right away?

4. What are some of the things Ivan dreams of?

5. At what point in the story do Ivan's feelings about his wife begin to change? Find the sentence in the text that supports your answer.

6. How does Ivan describe his wife's relatives?

7. What are your impressions of the ending of the story? Explain your answer.

8. At the beginning of the story, Ivan is described as a middle-class man who was "very well satisfied with his lot." How do his feelings about his life change when he considers the possibility of winning a large sum of money?

9. What do you think would have happened if Ivan and his wife had actually won the money?

10. What lesson can you learn from this story? Explain your answer.

Beyond the Lines

11. What would you do if you came into a large sum of money? Write a paragraph to describe what you see in your imagination.

12. People say that winning the lottery would not change who they are. Do you agree or disagree with this? Write a paragraph sharing your opinion on the subject.

13. Lotteries were banned in Canada in 1856, but were legalized once again in 1969. Do you think lotteries should still exist in the 21st century? Decide if you are for or against public lotteries. Provide arguments in support of your opinion.

Before Reading

1. Authors use different techniques to compare objects, people and places in their stories. A simile is a figure of speech in which the words *like* or *as* are used to make comparisons: for example, *He's as quiet as a mouse. I slept like a log.* Complete the similes below by matching each expression with the correct ending.

   1) As dark as   **a)** the inside of a cow

   2) As lively as   **b)** a post

   3) As deaf as   **c)** a doornail

   4) As numb as   **d)** a peg

   5) As dead as   **e)** a cricket

2. What do you already know about the author Stephen King?

3. Have you, or has someone you know ever been lost? Describe what happened.

4. What are some of the things that you fear the most?

While Reading

5. Make a list of all the similes you find while reading the story.

6. Who is Tom Gordon? Use information from the text to support your answer.

7. Where and when does the story take place? How does the setting help to create the mood of the story?

From *The Girl Who Loved Tom Gordon*

by Stephen King

T risha crawled out from under the tree-trunk, gasping and wincing. She was stiff everywhere from her tumble down the rocky slope, especially in her neck and left shoulder, and both her left arm and left leg—the limbs she
5 had been lying on—were asleep. Numb as pegs, her mother would have said. Grownups (at least the ones in her family) had a saying for everything: numb as a peg, happy as a lark, lively as a cricket, deaf as a post, dark as the inside of a cow, dead as a—

10 No, she didn't want to think of that one, not now.

Trisha tried to get on her feet, couldn't, and made her way into the little crescent of clearing at a hobbling crawl. As she moved, some of the feeling started to come back into her arm and leg—those unpleasant tingling bursts of
15 sensation. Needles and pins.

"Damn and blast," she croaked—mostly just to hear the sound of her own voice. "It's dark as the inside of a cow out here."

Except, as she stopped by the brook, Trisha realized that
20 it most surely wasn't. The little clearing was filled with moonlight, cold and lucid, strong enough to cast a firm

shadow beside her and put ash-bright sparkles on the water of her little stream. The object in the sky overhead was a slightly misshapen silver stone almost too bright to look
25 at . . . but she looked anyway, her swollen, itchy face and upcast eyes solemn. Tonight's moon was so bright that it had embarrassed all but the brightest stars into invisibility, and something about it, or about looking at it from where she was, made her feel how alone she was. Her earlier belief
30 that she would be saved just because Tom Gordon had gotten three outs in the top of the ninth was gone—might as well knock on wood, toss salt back over your shoulder, or make the sign of the cross before you stepped into the batter's box, as Nomar Garciaparra always did. There were
35 no cameras here, no instant replays, no cheering fans. The coldly beautiful face of the moon suggested to her that the Subaudible was more plausible after all, a God who didn't know He—or It— was a God, one with no interest in lost little girls, one with no real interest in anything, a knocked-
40 out-loaded God Whose mind was like a circling cloud of bugs and Whose eye was the **rapt** and vacant moon.

Trisha bent over the stream to splash her throbbing face, saw her reflection, and moaned. The wasp-sting above her left cheekbone had swelled some more (perhaps she
45 had scratched it or bumped it in her sleep), bursting through the mud she had smeared on it like a newly awakened volcano bursting through the old caked lava of its last eruption. It had mashed her eye out of shape, making it all crooked and freakish, the sort of eye that
50 made you glance away if you saw it floating toward you—usually in the face of a mentally retarded person—on the street. The rest of her face was as bad or even worse: lumpy where she had been stung, merely swollen where mosquitoes in their hundreds had had at her while she was
55 sleeping. The water by the bank where she crouched was relatively still, and in it she saw there was at least one mosquito still on her. It clung to the corner of her right eye, too **logy** to even pull its **proboscis** from her flesh. Another of those grownup sayings occurred to her: too
60 stuffed to jump.

She struck at it and it burst, filling her eye with her own blood, making it sting. Trisha managed not to scream, but a wavery sound of revulsion—*mmmmmmhh*—escaped her tightly pressed lips. She looked unbelievingly at the blood on her fingers. That one mosquito could hold so much! No one would believe it!

She dipped her cupped hands into the water and washed her face. She didn't drink any, vaguely remembering someone saying that woods-water could make you sick, but the feel of it on her hot and lumpy skin was wonderful—like cold satin. She dipped up more, wetting her neck and soaking her arms to the elbow: Then she scooped up mud and began to apply it—not just on the bites this time but all over, from the round collar of her 36 GORDON shirt right up to the roots of her hair.

As she did it she thought of an *I Love Lucy* episode she'd seen on Nick at Nite, Lucy and Ethel at the beauty parlor, both of them wearing these funky 1958 mudpacks, and Desi had come in and looked from one woman

VOCABULARY

logy: lethargic

proboscis: the long part of an animal or insect's head

rapt: full of emotion

to the other and he had said, "Hey Loocy, jwich one are jew?" and the audience had **howled**. She probably looked
85 like that, but Trisha didn't care. There was no audience out here, no laugh-track, either, and she couldn't stand to be bitten anymore. It would drive her crazy if she was.

She applied mud for five minutes, finishing with a couple of careful dabs to the eyelids, then bent over to look
90 at her reflection. What she saw in the relatively still water by the bank was a minstrel-show mudgirl by moonlight. Her face was a **pasty** gray, like a face on a vase pulled out of some archaeological dig. Above it her hair stood up in a filthy spout. Her eyes were white and wet and frightened.
95 She didn't look funny, like Lucy and Ethel getting their beauty treatments. She looked dead. Dead and badly inbarned, or whatever they called it.

Speaking to the face in the water, Trisha intoned: "*Then Little Black Sambo said, 'Please, tigers, do not take my fine
100 new clothes.'*"

But that wasn't funny, either. She smeared mud up her lumpy, itchy arms, then lowered her hands toward the water, meaning to wash them off. But that was stupid. The goshdamn old bugs would just bite her there.

105 The pins and needles had mostly worked out of her arm and leg; Trisha was able to squat and pee without falling over. She was also able to stand up and walk, although she grimaced with pain each time she moved her head more than a little to the right or left. She supposed she had a kind
110 of whiplash injury, like the one Mrs. Chetwynd from up the block had gotten when some old man had rammed her car from behind as she waited for a traffic light to change. The old man hadn't been hurt a bit, but poor Mrs. Chetwynd had been in a neck brace for six weeks. Maybe
115 they would put *her* in a neck brace when she got out of this. Maybe they would take her to a hospital in a helicopter with a red cross on the belly like in *M*A*S*H*, and—

Forget it, Trisha. It was the scary cold voice. *No neck brace for you. No helicopter ride, either.*
120 "Shut up," she muttered, but the voice wouldn't.

You won't even get inbarned because they're never going to find you. You'll die out here, just wander around in these woods

until you die, and the animals will come and eat your rotting
body and some day some hunter will come along and find your
125 *bones.*

There was something so terribly plausible about this
last—she had heard similar stories on the TV news not just
once but several times, it seemed—that she began to cry
again. She could actually see the hunter, a man in a bright
130 red woolen jacket and an orange cap, a man who needed a
shave. Looking for a place to lie up and wait for a deer or
maybe just wanting to take a leak. He sees something white
and thinks at first, *Just a stone,* but as he gets closer he sees
that the stone has eyesockets.

135 "Stop it," she whispered, walking back to the fallen tree
and the wrinkled spread remains of the poncho under it
(she hated the poncho now; she didn't know why, but it
seemed to symbolize everything that had gone wrong).
"Stop it, please."

140 The cold voice would not. The cold voice had one more
thing to say. One more thing, at least.

Or maybe you won't just die. Maybe the thing out there will
kill you and eat you.

Trisha stopped by the fallen tree—one hand reached
145 out and grasped the dead **jut** of a small branch—and
looked around nervously. From the moment of waking all
she'd really been able to think about was how badly she
itched. The mud had now soothed the worst of the itching
and the residual throb of the wasp-stings, and she again
150 realized where she was: in the woods alone and at night.

"At least there's a moon," she said, standing by the tree
and looking nervously around her little crescent of **clearing**.
It looked even smaller now, as
if the trees and underbrush had
155 crept in closer while she was
sleeping. Crept in *slyly.*

The moonlight wasn't as
good a thing as she'd thought,
either. It was bright in the
160 clearing, true, but it was a
deceptive brightness that made
everything look simultaneously

From *The Girl Who Loved Tom Gordon* **23**

too real and not real at all. Shadows were too black, and when a breeze stirred the trees, the shadows changed in a disquieting way.

Something twitted in the woods, seemed to choke, twitted again, and was silent.

An owl hooted, far off.

Closer to, a branch snapped.

What was that? Trisha thought, turning toward the snapping sound. Her heartbeat began to ramp up from a walk to a jog to a run. In another few seconds it would be sprinting and then *she* might be sprinting as well, panicked all over again and running like a deer in front of a forest fire.

"Nothing, it was nothing," she said. Her voice was low and rapid . . . very much her mother's voice, although she did not know this. Nor did she know that in a motel room thirty miles from where Trisha stood by the fallen tree, her mother had sat up out of a troubled sleep, still half-dreaming with her eyes open, sure that something awful had happened to her lost daughter, or was about to happen.

It's the thing you hear, Trisha, said the cold voice. Its tone was sad on top, unspeakably **gleeful** underneath. *It's coming for you. It's got your scent.*

"There is no *thing*," Trisha said in a desperate, whispery voice that broke into complete silence each time it wavered upward. "Come on, give me a break, there is no *thing*."

190 The unreliable moonlight had changed the shapes of the trees, had turned them into bone faces with black eyes. The sound of two branches rubbing together became the clotted croon of a monster. Trisha turned in a clumsy circle, trying to look everywhere at once, her eyes rolling in her 195 muddy face.

It's a special *thing, Trisha—the thing that waits for the lost ones. It lets them wander until they're good and scared—because fear makes them taste better, it sweetens the flesh—and then it comes for them. You'll see it. It'll come out of the trees any* 200 *minute now. A matter of seconds, really. And when you see its face you'll go insane. If there was anyone to hear you, they'd think you were screaming. But you'll be laughing, won't you? Because that's what insane people do when their lives are ending, they laugh . . . and they laugh . . . and they laugh.*

205 "Stop it, there is no thing, there is no thing in the woods, you stop it!"

She whispered this very fast, and the hand holding the **nub** of dead branch clutched it tighter and tighter until it broke with a loud report like a starter's gun. The sound 210 made her jump and utter a little scream, but it also steadied her. She knew what it was, after all just a branch, and one *she* had broken. She could still break branches, she still had that much control over the world. Sounds were just sounds. Shadows were just shadows. She could be afraid, 215 she could listen to that stupid traitor of a voice if she wanted to, but there was no

(thing special thing)

in the woods. There was *wildlife,* and there was undoubtedly a spot of the old kill-or-be-killed going on out 220 there at this very second, but there was no crea—

There is.

And there was.

Now, stopping all of her thoughts and holding her breath 225 without realizing it, Trisha knew with a simple cold certainty that

VOCABULARY

gleeful: full of joy
nub: a small piece

there was. There was *something.* Inside her there were at that moment no voices, only a part of her she didn't understand, a special set of **eclipsed** nerves that perhaps
230 slept in the world of houses and phones and electric lights and came fully alive only out here in the woods. That part didn't see and couldn't think, but it could feel. Now it felt something in the woods.

"Hello?" she called toward the moonlight-and-bone
235 faces of the trees. "Hello, is someone there?"

VOCABULARY

eclipsed: hidden

After Reading

1. Respond to the text using **three** of the prompts below.

   - *I enjoyed this story because . . .*
   - *The main ch*____ *risha, . . .*
   - *when Trisha . . . because . . .*
   - *ke that, I would . . .*
   - *read the rest of this story because . . .*

   a is? Find information in the text to

   into this situation?

   ink about the ending of the simile

5. ____ *y cold voice"* represents?

6. ____ the cold voice say that scares Trisha and makes her cry?

7. What do you know about Trisha's mother?

8. Why, all of a sudden, is Trisha so certain that there is something in the woods? What do you think "the thing" in the woods could be?

9. Personification is a technique used in literature to give human qualities and characteristics to objects or animals. Find two examples of personification in the story.

10. Make a list of words and phrases in the story that describe Trisha's fear as she fights to survive in the woods.

11. Do you think that Trisha has what it takes to survive her ordeal in the woods? Why or why not?

Beyond the Lines

12. The main character in this story is lost in the woods, injured, alone and afraid. Describe a situation that would be *your* worst nightmare.

13. Continue the story, imitating the author's style (use of italics, similes, personification, conflict, etc.). Begin your story with the following sentence: *"Hello?" she called toward the moonlight-and-bone faces of the trees. "Hello, is someone there?"*

Before Reading

1. Make a list of as many advertising slogans as you can think of. Use your imagination to complete the following slogan: _____: We Want to Be Your Only _____ .

2. What do crows usually represent?

While Reading

3. Draw a T-chart like the one shown below. Complete the first column of the chart. While you read the story, complete the second column.

Crows	
Symbol	Meaning

4. An author's style is what makes his or her writing unique. The choice of words and how the author uses language shows his or her personality and attitude toward a subject. Author Ian Frazier is known for his humorous style of writing. List some examples of humour while you read the story and explain why you find them funny.

Tomorrow's Bird

by Ian Frazier

S ince May, I've been working for the crows, and so far it's
the best job I ever had. I kind of fell into it by a
combination of preparedness and luck. I'd been casting
around a bit, looking for a new direction in my career, and
5 one afternoon when I was out on my walk I happened to
see some crows fly by. One of them landed on a telephone
wire just above my head. I looked at him for a moment,
and then on impulse I made a *skchhh* noise with my teeth
and lips. He seemed to like that; I saw his tail make a quick
10 upward bobbing motion at the sound. Encouraged, I made
the noise again, and again his tail bobbed. He looked at me
closely with one eye, then turned his beak and looked at
me with the other, meanwhile readjusting his feet on the
wire. After a few minutes, he cawed and flew off to join his
15 companions. I had a good feeling I couldn't put into words.
Basically, I thought the meeting had gone well, and as it
turned out, I was right. When I got home there was a
message from the crows saying I had the job.

That first interview proved indicative of the crows'
20 business style. They are very informal and relaxed, unlike
their public persona, and mostly they leave me alone. I'm

given a general direction of what they want done, but the specifics of how to do it are up to me. For example, the crows have long been unhappy about public misperceptions of them: that they raid other birds' nests, drive songbirds away, eat garbage and dead things, can't sing, etc., all of which are completely untrue once you know them. My first task was to take these misperceptions and turn them into a more positive image. I decided the crows needed a slogan that emphasized their strengths as a species. The slogan I came up with was "Crows: We Want To Be Your Only Bird.™" I told this to the crows, they loved it, and we've been using it ever since.

Crows speak a dialect of English rather like that of the remote hill people of the **Alleghenies**. If you're not accustomed to it, it can be hard to understand. In their formal speech they are as measured and clear as a radio announcer from the Midwest—though, as I say, they are seldom formal with me. (For everyday needs, of course, they caw.) Their unit of money is the empty soda bottle, which trades at a rate of about twenty to the dollar. In the recent years of economic boom, the crows have quietly amassed great power. With investment capital based on their nationwide control of everything that gets run over on the roads, they have bought a number of major companies. Pepsi-Cola is now owned by the crows, as well as Knight Ridder Newspapers and the company that makes Tombstone Frozen Pizzas. The New York Metropolitan Opera is now **wholly** crow-owned.

In order to stay competitive, as most people know, the crows recently merged with the **ravens**. This was done not only for reasons of growth but also to better serve those millions who live and work near crows. In the future, both crows and ravens will be known by the group name of Crows, so if you see a bird and wonder which it is, you don't have to waste any time: officially and legally, it's a crow. The net result of this, of course, is that now there are a lot more crows—which is exactly what the crows want. Studies they've sponsored show that there could be anywhere from ten to a thousand times more crows than there already are, with no strain on carrying capacity.

A healthy increase in crow numbers would make basic services like cawing loudly outside your bedroom window at six in the morning available to all. In this area, as in many others, the crows are thinking very long-term.

If more people in the future get a chance to know crows as I have done, they are in for a real treat. Because I must say, the crows have been absolutely wonderful to me. I like them not just as highly profitable business associates but as friends. Their aggressive side, admittedly quite strong in disputes with **scarlet tanagers**, etc., has been nowhere in evidence around me. I could not wish for any companions more charming. The other day I was having lunch with an important crow in the park, me sipping from a drinking fountain while he ate peanuts taken from a squirrel. In between sharp downward raps of his **bill** on the peanut shell to poke it open, he drew me out with seemingly **artless** questions. Sometimes the wind would push the shell to one side and he would steady it with one large foot while continuing the raps with his beak. And all the while, he kept up his attentive questioning, making me feel that, business considerations aside, he was truly interested in what I had to say.

"CROWS: WE WANT To Be Your Only Bird.™" I think this slogan is worth repeating, because there's a lot behind it.

VOCABULARY

Alleghenies: a mountain range in the United States

artless: simple

bill: a bird's beak

raven: a large black bird

scarlet tanager: a bird with bright red feathers and black wings and tail

wholly: entirely

Of course, the crows don't literally want (or expect) to be the only species of bird left on the planet. They admire and
95 enjoy other kinds of birds and even hope that there will still be some remaining in limited numbers out of doors as well as in zoos and museums.

But in terms of daily usage, the crows hope that you will think of them first when you're looking for those
100 quality-of-life intangibles usually associated with birds. Singing, for example: crows actually can sing, and beautifully, too; however, so far they have not been given any chance. In the future, with fewer other birds around, they feel that they will be.

105 Whether they're good-naturedly harassing an owl caught out in daylight, or carrying bits of sticks and used gauze bandage in their beaks to make their colorful, freeform nests, or simply landing on the sidewalk in front of you with their characteristic double hop, the crows have
110 become a part of the fabric of our days. When you had your first kiss, the crows were there, flying around nearby. They were cawing overhead at your college graduation, and worrying a hamburger wrapper through the wire mesh of a

trash container in front of the building when you went in
for your first job interview, and flapping past the door of
the hospital where you held your firstborn child. The crows
have always been with us, and they promise that by
growing the species at a predicted rate of 17 percent a year,
in the future they'll be around even more.

The crows aren't the last Siberian tigers, and they don't
pretend to be. They're not interested in being a part of
anybody's dying tradition. But then how many of us deal
with Siberian tigers on a regular basis? Usually, the nontech
stuff we deal with, besides humans, is squirrels, pigeons,
raccoons, rats, mice, and a few kinds of bugs. The crows are
confident enough to claim that they will be able to
compete effectively even with these familiar and **well-
entrenched** providers. Indeed, they have already begun to
displace pigeons in the category of walking around under
park benches with chewing gum stuck to their feet.
Scampering nervously in attics, sneaking through pet
doors, and **gnawing** little holes in things are all in the
crows' expansion plans.

I would not have taken this job if I did not believe,
strongly and deeply, in the crows myself. And I do. I could
go on and on about the crow's generosity, taste in music,
sense of family values; the "buddy system" they invented
to use against other birds, the work they do for the
Shriners, and more. But they're paying me a lot of bottles
to say this—I can't expect everybody to believe me. I do
ask, if you're unconvinced, that you take this simple test:
next time you're looking out a window or driving in a car,
notice if there's a crow in sight. Then multiply that one
crow by lots and lots of crows, and you'll get an idea of
what the next years will bring. In the bird department, no
matter what, the future is going
to be almost all crows, almost all
the time. That's just a fact.

So why not just accept it,
and learn to appreciate it, as so
many of us have already? The
crows are going to influence
our culture and our world in

115
120
125
130
135
140
145
150

VOCABULARY
gnawing: chewing
scampering: running quickly
well-entrenched: strong

beneficial ways we can't even imagine today. Much of what they envision I am not yet at liberty to disclose, but I can tell you that it is magnificent. They are going to be birds like we've never seen. In their dark, jewel-like eyes burns an ambition to be more and better and to fly around all over the place constantly. They're smart, they're driven, and they're comin' at us. The crows: let's get ready to welcome tomorrow's only bird.

After Reading

1. How did the author of the story get the job working for the crows?

2. What are some public misconceptions about crows?

3. How do the crows adapt their speech to communicate in formal and informal situations?

4. What happened to the ravens?

5. What personality traits do crows display?

6. Find a sentence in the text that proves the crows want to dominate the planet.

7. What are some everyday actions that the crows hope to perform?

8. Read the five facts about crows listed below. Find an example in the story to support each one.

   a) Crows are highly intelligent creatures.

   b) Crows can be found everywhere around the world.

   c) Some crows have been taught to count and to imitate human speech.

   d) Crows can produce a wide variety of calls.

   e) Crows have an aggressive personality.

9. Personification is a technique used in literature to give human qualities and characteristics to objects or animals. List at least three examples of personification in the story.

10. The crows' advertising slogan is "Crows: We Want to Be Your Only Bird." In what ways do the crows plan on taking over the jobs of other animals?

11. What do you think the crows in the story symbolize or represent? Support your answer with information from the text.

Beyond the Lines

12. Although the story is written in a humorous tone, it leaves the readers with something to think about. What message do you think the author is trying to share with you? What lesson can you learn from this story?

13. Use information from the story to write a sales pitch for "tomorrow's bird" from the crow's point of view.

14. Imagine you were hired to create an advertising campaign to promote a particular animal. Which animal would you choose to promote and what would your slogan be?

William Bell was born in Toronto, Ontario, in 1945. He has taught English in high schools as well as universities, and has written more than a dozen books for young adults. His novel *The Blue Helmet* won the Canadian Librarian's Association Young Adult Book of the Year award for 2007, and his other award-winning works include the novels *Forbidden City* and *Crabbe.* Bell is known for his ability to write from the perspectives of teenagers dealing with difficulties ranging from the simple to the extreme.

Before Reading

1. Match each of the following expressions with its meaning.

   a) to be sick and tired
   b) to be on the house
   c) to skate around in circles
   d) to be on the outside looking in
   e) to be a mixed blessing
   f) to take a stroll

   1) to go for a leisurely walk
   2) to have advantages and disadvantages
   3) to be very discouraged
   4) to be provided free of charge
   5) to make no progress
   6) to be excluded from a group or activity

2. Have you ever been in a situation where you feel like you don't belong, as if you were on the outside looking in? Explain your answer.

While Reading

3. Read the first two paragraphs of the story. From the information provided in this passage, how would you describe the narrator of the story?

4. Make a chart like the one below. List the characters mentioned in the story and provide at least one piece of information about each person.

Characters in *The Blue Helmet*	
Name	Information (thoughts, speech, actions)

5. As you read, write down ten new words or expressions from the story. Provide a definition for each one.

From *The Blue Helmet*

by William Bell

I was relaxing in my booth, taking a break and letting my thoughts wander while the breakfast crowd got their caffeine and sugar fixes. Around me, the tinkle of spoons on saucers and cups, the grumble of conversation, the
5 rustle of newspapers. The tables along the opposite wall were full, and everyone was reading the news. At one point, as if they had rehearsed it, almost all of them held their newspapers open at the same time, making a sort of billboard, each black-and-white patch floating between a
10 pair of hands. A headline shouted that someone whose name I couldn't pronounce was on trial for war crimes in a city I had never heard of. A picture showed a man in a suit standing behind a podium, with a big sloppy grin on his face. Underneath, it said, GABLER ANNOUNCES
15 ENVIRONMENTAL INITIATIVE. There was a story about the Sudan and Africa. An airline had gone bankrupt. And then, as people turned a page or shifted in their seats, the billboard broke up.

I pushed my half-eaten muffin away. I had never heard
20 of Gabler or the man on trial, didn't know what the Sudan was, knew nothing about Africa or the airline. I couldn't

have felt more empty-headed if the readers of the morning papers had stood by my table and peppered me with questions. And suddenly I was ambushed by a familiar 25 image—me, on the outside of a building, looking through a locked window into a comfortable room. People relaxing around an open fire, laughing and talking together, people who understood how the world worked.

I was sick and tired of not knowing things. I shifted my 30 eyes to the two guys by the café door, elbows on the table, heads together, the bills of their caps almost touching, then the students packed into the booth beside mine, arguing energetically about some book they were studying. Naturally, I hadn't read the book. Naturally, I hadn't even 35 heard of it.

In high school, as far as I went, I got through my courses without much effort, collecting credits the way you'd pick up stale food you really didn't want in the cafeteria. But at the same time, although I never admitted 40 it to myself, I always felt I was missing something. I knew I wasn't stupid.

I was ignorant.

Not exactly a **cheery** conclusion to come to. Not exactly a morale booster. But I had to admit it was true.

Why today? What had brought this on, the way you realize you've got frostbite only when your **flesh** begins to sting? Was it being around Cutter the brain so much, with his books and computers and far-our theories? Or Andrea, running her own business? Or Abe, with his weather maps and charts and storm-tracking software? Was it because Cutter was persuaded his work was important and Abe was having so much fun?

The next time I took Cutter's books back to the library—not overdue this time—and handed them in at the returns desk, I stood looking around at the ranks of shelves, the row of computers, the magazine rack. In grade nine we had had a library orientation class to teach us how the place operated and how to find stuff, but as usual I hadn't paid much attention. I didn't know what I wanted anyway. I was hopeless.

I turned to go. Behind me, I heard, "Can I help you find something?"

The guy on the other side of the desk looked more like a janitor than a librarian—**rumpled** jeans, baggy sweatshirt, a screwdriver in one hand, a stapler in the other. A pen hung from a cord around his neck. The cord was caught on a name tag that said CLANCY.

"Um, well, I was sort of looking for—" what? I had no idea. "A good book," I said stupidly.

Clancy looked me up and down. He figures I'm a bonehead, I thought.

"Why not try our Perennial Favourites table?" he said, pointing across the room with the screwdriver. "Over there. Call me if you need help." He went back to trying to unjam the stapler.

Wondering what "perennial" meant, I took a look at the display, just so Clancy wouldn't think I was a complete idiot. About two dozen books had been placed on wire racks so their covers were easily visible. I picked a few up, riffled the pages, put them back. Then I spotted a really thin one. *The Old Man and the Sea* it was called.

A kiddie book. I flipped it open to the first page. *He was an old man who fished alone in a skiff on the Gulf Stream and he had gone eighty-four days now without taking a fish.* Didn't sound like a kid's story.

I checked the book out, took it back to my room, and tossed it onto the table beside my bed. Maybe I'd read it, maybe I'd just hold onto it for a while and return it to the library. Later that afternoon, I was in Andrea's drugstore to pick up a delivery to Mrs. Waslynchuck, a **pensioner** who lived alone unless you counted the four cats in an apartment on 33rd Street. In a rack of magazines and crossword puzzle books I saw a paperback, *Increase Your Word Power! Add one word per day to your vocabulary! That's 365 new, useful words each year!* the cover said. Well, they can count, anyway, I thought, bending to replace the book. Then I changed my mind.

"I'd like to buy this," I told Andrea as I stuffed the little bag of Mrs. Waslynchuck's pills into my **pannier**.

"No way," she replied.

"Huh?"

"On the house," Andrea said, smiling. "Enjoy."

"Looks like we have a new customer," Reena said as I pushed through the door into the café kitchen. She was adding up the lunch receipts at a little table in the corner, a half-eaten sandwich and a glass of milk beside her calculator. "Andrea recommended him to us. He lives on 13th. Bruce something."

"Cutter?" I said. "He's ordering take-out?"

She tilted her head toward a brown bag on the counter under the phone. The top was folded over and the bill stapled to it. "Cold chicken sandwich and a tub of salad. An older fella, is he?"

"Thirties, maybe. In there somewhere."

"Sounded a little strange on the phone."

"Yup, that's Cutter all right," I replied, picking up the bag and heading for the back door.

Garbage bins and recycling boxes overflowing with cans and bottles stood like sentries along the curb on 13th street. Pickup day. As I walked up Cutter's sidewalk,

William Bell

pushing the tank, the curtain at the front window **twitched**. I rang the bell, stepped back and made a face at the camera.

"Come on in, Lee."

Locks clicked and clacked. Cutter held the vestibule door open for me. "How are you?" he said pleasantly.

He led the way back to the kitchen. "Got time for a cup of tea?" he asked. "It's all ready." Cups, milk and sugar, and a teapot had been set out.

"I guess so."

"Help yourself. Have you eaten?"

"Yeah." I filled the mugs with coal-black tea. I wondered how long it had been brewing.

"Mind if I go ahead?" he asked, ripping open the bag. "I'm starved. I don't always have a very good appetite."

"No problem," I said, and sipped my tea. It was strong enough to dissolve the enamel off my teeth.

Cutter seemed calm. His hair was combed, and he was wearing khakis and a cardigan over a white shirt. As if he was going to class. Not that I'd know how university students dressed. He ate slowly, forking the salad directly from the plastic container, taking small bites from the sandwich. His eye wasn't twitching today.

Then he jumped up and scooted through to the office. I craned my neck to see what he was up to. He was bent over, holding the **drape** back a little, peering out the front window as if he didn't want to be seen. He stood up and returned to his chair and took a bite from the sandwich.

"What's up?" I asked.

"Oh, just checking, just checking." I waited. "The garbage," he said.

"Oh."

"Well, you know. Making sure no one is messing with it. Taking it."

"You're worried someone will take your garbage?"

"Yeah."

VOCABULARY

drape: curtain

pannier: a large basket

pensioner: a person who lives on a pension

twitched: moved with a sudden motion

From *The Blue Helmet* 41

165   This is going to be one of those Cutter conversations where we skate around in circles, I thought, holding back a laugh. I didn't know 170 whether I should humour him and keep talking, or let it go. But *not* talking would insult him, in a way. As if I thought he was a child and his 175 conversation worthless.

"Isn't that why you put it out? To be trucked away?"

"No. Yes. I mean, take as in rob."

"Who would steal garbage?"

"They can find out everything about you by examining 180 what comes out the back door," he explained. "That's why I use that big machine in the office. But even **shredded** paper can be reconstructed, I suppose."

It was hard to imagine a ring of trash thieves terrorizing the neighbourhood, but he was right, in a way. In the 185 movies, cops and spies often **scrounged** through trash for information.

"They look for records, right?" I said. "Phone bills, credit card statements, and stuff."

"Right," Cutter replied, his face brightening. "You can 190 construct a very reliable profile of a household by analyzing what they throw away. Our garbage is a mirror of our lives. Only with mayonnaise or peanut butter smears on it." He smiled, pleased at his joke.

"On the other hand, They already know everything 195 about us. We live in an electronic wonderland. Most people have at least two bank credit cards, plus ones for gasoline, department stores, and so on. They don't realize it, but all those corps exchange information about their clients. A lot of them sell the information to marketing companies. 200 That's where targeted junk mail comes from. There's no such thing as privacy."

If Cutter was aware that he was contradicting himself, he didn't show it. If he was right, why would anyone need to go through his garbage? But the more I was with him, the more I saw that being consistent wasn't part of the way his mind worked.

He popped the last bit of sandwich in his mouth and scrunched up the bag. "Feel like a walk?"

"You mean outside?"

"Of course. Just let me get my jacket."

I didn't mind going. It was entertaining, listening to his way-out theories, probably because they had a certain amount of truth to them—or sounded as if they did.

On the verandah, Cutter looked around, then **plucked** a hair from his head. He licked his fingers, ran the hair through the spit, and pressed it across the crack between the door and the frame.

"If anybody sneaks in while we're gone—"

"You'll be able to tell."

"Exactly."

I didn't mention the back door.

On the way down the street, Cutter's eyes darted from side to side. Every few steps he looked over his shoulder. Then he stopped as if he'd forgotten something.

"I've got to quit doing this," he said, and started walking again.

I wondered if he'd wanted to take a stroll because he was planning to tell me more conspiracies and he figured his house was bugged. I shook my head. You're getting paranoid, too, I told myself. Cut it out.

Around the corner of 13th and Lakeshore Drive, we passed through a gate in the high chain-link fence and entered the park. The lake was calm and slate-grey, the sky clear, the air chilly. To the west, the stacks of the Lakeview power generating station stood out against the sky. We walked along the bike path, stepping aside for rollerbladers and people pushing strollers.

"This whole park," Cutter said, **ambling** along, his shoulders hunched, his hands jammed into his pockets, "used to be a hospital for the mentally

VOCABULARY
ambling: walking slowly
plucked: pulled out
shredded: cut into small pieces
scrounged: looked through

infirm. I read up on it after I moved here. It was actually a farm, and the inmates, the ones not locked down, grew vegetables and fruit. The idea was for the institution to be as self-sustaining as possible so it didn't put too much **burden** on taxpayers. And experts in those days thought hard work was good for the patients. A lot of them were mentally retarded—the patients, that is. Then attitudes changed and drugs came along—a mixed blessing, believe me. Most of the inmates were released to other facilities, or onto the street."

I thought of the Queen of Sweden and a few of the other astronauts who sat in the café in the mornings.

"The psychiatric hospital shut down," Cutter went on. "For a few years the buildings and grounds were rented out to movie companies and TV shows. Then the college took over most of the buildings and fixed them up."

He stopped and looked around. "I like to visit sometimes and sort of **commune** with the ghosts of the crazy people who used to live here."

He didn't say it, but I figured he was thinking that at one time he would have been one of the inmates, locked in a room behind bars, listening to the screamers as he tried to sleep.

"It's not much fun being crazy," he said, kicking a stone on the path.

I couldn't think of anything to reply to that, so we walked in silence. I was feeling a little guilty, coming along because I thought Cutter might say something funny—to me, not to him.

"You're a big help to me, Lee," he said after a while. Which made me feel more guilty.

"Me? How? All I do is bring you your prescriptions and stuff."

"You just are."

After Reading

1. How old do you think Lee is? Find information in the story to support your answer.

2. How does Lee feel different from other people? What separates him from them?

3. What reason does the narrator offer for the sudden realization of his ignorance?

4. Did Lee enjoy the time he spent in high school? Explain your answer using information from the text.

5. What are some ways in which Lee tries to make himself less ignorant?

6. Describe the relationship between Cutter and Lee. Use the following questions for help. *How do they know each other? In what ways does Lee help Cutter? What does Lee think about Cutter's behaviour?*

7. What symptoms of paranoia does Cutter display?

8. When Cutter asks Lee if he feels like a walk, Lee asks, "You mean outside?" Why do you think Lee asks this?

9. Why does Cutter stick a hair between the door and the frame?

10. Cutter says, "It's not much fun being crazy." Do you think Cutter is referring to himself when he says this? Do you think he really is crazy? Explain your answer.

11. Why do you think Cutter feels that Lee is a big help to him?

Beyond the Lines

12. Lee is in conflict with his ignorance and is searching for a way to solve this conflict. He is looking for peace within himself. Cutter also faces his own internal conflicts. How might Lee and Cutter be considered "blue helmets" to each other?

13. Lee managed to get through his courses in high school "without much effort" yet he still feels ignorant. What do you think is the difference between being ignorant and being stupid? What important lessons about life cannot be learned in school?

14. Cutter believes that he is constantly being watched. Do you think people in today's society are more at risk for invasion of privacy? Explain your answer.

ABOUT THE AUTHOR

Grace Paley (1922–2007), an American short story writer, poet and activist, was born in the Bronx, New York, and was raised by her Russian-Jewish immigrant parents to support peace and social justice. She went to university at the age of 15, and studied with the poet W. H. Auden, but she is known mostly for her short stories, many of which reflected her views on human rights and her anti-war stance. *Enormous Changes at the Last Minute* is her best known collection of short stories.

Before Reading

1. Read the expressions below. Write the meaning of each one.

   a) to be born out of wedlock

   b) to be of small/great consequence

   c) to keep an eye on

   d) to keep your wits about you

   e) to have the last word

   f) to look something in the face

2. What elements are necessary to make a good short story?

3. Using the story starter below, brainstorm ideas for a short story. Write for five minutes without stopping. Write as much as you can in the time you have.

   "Once in my time, there was a woman and she had a son."

4. What elements listed in question 2 did you include in your story? What elements are missing?

While Reading

5. Compare the story you wrote in question 3 with the narrator's story in lines 26 to 35 on page 48.

6. Pay attention to the narrator of this story. Decide if the narrator is a man or a woman. Explain your answer.

7. What can you learn about story writing from reading this story?

A Conversation With My Father

by Grace Paley

M y father is eighty-six years old and in bed. His heart, that bloody motor, is equally old and will not do certain jobs anymore. It still floods his head with brainy light. But it won't let his legs carry the weight of his body
5 around the house. Despite my metaphors, this muscle failure is not due to his old heart, he says, but to a potassium shortage. Sitting on one pillow, leaning on three, he offers last-minute advice and makes a request.

"I would like you to write a simple story just once
10 more," he says, "the kind de Maupassant wrote, or Chekhov, the kind you used to write. Just recognizable people and then write down what happened to them next."

I say, "Yes, why not? That's possible." I want to please
15 him, though I don't remember writing that way. I *would* like to try to tell such a story, if he means the kind that begins: "There was a woman . . ." followed by plot, the absolute line between two points which I've always despised. Not for literary reasons, but because it takes all
20 hope away. Everyone, real or invented, deserves the open destiny of life.

Finally I thought of a story that had been happening for a couple of years right across the street. I wrote it down, then read it aloud. "Pa," I said, "how about this? Do you
25 mean something like this?"

Once in my time there was a woman and she had a son. They lived nicely, in a small apartment in Manhattan. This boy at about fifteen became a **junkie**, which is not unusual in our neighbourhood. In order to
30 maintain her close friendship with him, she became a junkie too. She said it was part of the youth culture, with which she felt very much at home. After a while, for a number of reasons, the boy gave it all up and left the city and his mother in disgust. Hopeless and alone, she
35 **grieved**. We all visit her.

"O.K., Pa, that's it," I said, "an **unadorned** and miserable tale."

"But that's not what I mean," my father said. "You misunderstood me on purpose. You know there's a lot more
40 to it. You know that. You left everything out. Turgenev wouldn't do that. Chekhov wouldn't do that. There are in fact Russian writers you never heard of, you don't have an **inkling** of, as good as anyone, who can write a plain ordinary story, who would not leave out what you have left
45 out. I object not to facts but to people sitting in trees talking senselessly, voices from who knows where . . ."

"Forget that one, Pa, what have I left out now? In this one?"

"Her looks, for instance."
50 "Oh. Quite **handsome**, I think. Yes."

"Her hair?"

"Dark, with heavy braids, as though she were a girl or a foreigner."

"What were her parents like, her stock? That she
55 became such a person. It's interesting, you know."

"From out of town. Professional people. The first to be divorced in their county. How's that? Enough?" I asked.

"With you, it's all a joke," he said. "What about the boy's father? Why didn't you mention him? Who was he?
60 Or was the boy born out of **wedlock**?"

"Yes," I said. "He was born out of wedlock."

"For Godsakes, doesn't anyone in your stories get married? Doesn't anyone have the time to run down to City Hall before they jump into bed?"

65 "No," I said. "In real life, yes. But in my stories, no."

"Why do you answer me like that?"

"Oh Pa, this is a simple story about a smart woman who came to N.Y.C. full of interest love trust excitement very up to date, and about her son, what a hard time she had in this
70 world. Married or not, it's of small consequence."

"It is of great consequence," he said.

"O.K.," I said.

"O.K. O.K. yourself," he said, "but listen. I believe you that
75 she's good-looking, but I don't think she was so smart."

"That's true," I said. "Actually, that's the trouble with stories. People start out fantastic. You
80 think they're extraordinary, but it turns out as the work goes along, they're just average with a good education. Sometimes the other way around, the person's a

85 kind of dumb innocent, but he **outwits** you and you can't even think of an ending good enough."

"What do you do then?"
90 he asked. He had been a doctor for a couple of decades and then an artist for a couple of decades and he's still interested in details,
95 craft, technique.

"Well, you just have to let the story lie around till some agreement can be reached between you and the stubborn hero."

"Aren't you talking silly, now?" he asked. "Start again,"
100 he said. "It so happens I'm not going out this evening. Tell the story again. See what you can do this time."

"O.K.," I said. "But it's not a five-minute job." Second attempt:

Once, across the street from us, there was a fine
105 handsome woman, our neighbour. She had a son whom she loved because she'd known him since birth (in helpless chubby infancy, and in the wrestling, hugging ages, seven to ten, as well as earlier and later). This boy, when he fell into the fist of adolescence, became a junkie. He was not
110 a hopeless one. He was in fact hopeful, an **ideologue** and successful converter. With his busy brilliance, he wrote persuasive articles for his high-school newspaper. Seeking a wider audience, using important connections, he drummed into Lower Manhattan newsstand
115 distribution a periodical called *Oh! Golden Horse!*

In order to keep him from feeling guilty (because guilt is the stony heart of nine tenths of all clinically diagnosed cancers in America today, she said), and because she had always believed in giving bad habits
120 room at home where one could keep an eye on them, she too became a junkie. Her kitchen was famous for a while—a center for intellectual addicts who knew what they were doing. A few felt artistic like Coleridge and others were scientific and revolutionary like Leary.

Although she was often high herself, certain good mothering reflexes remained, and she saw to it that there was lots of orange juice around and honey and milk and vitamin pills. However, she never cooked anything but chili, and that no more than once a week. She explained, when we talked to her, seriously, with neighborly concern, that it was her part in the youth culture and she would rather be with the young, it was an honor, than with her own generation.

One week, while nodding through an Antonioni film, this boy was severely jabbed by the elbow of a **stern** and **proselytizing** girl, sitting beside him. She offered immediate apricots and nuts for his sugar level, spoke to him sharply, and took him home.

She heard of him and his work and she herself published, edited, and wrote a competitive journal called *Man Does Live by Bread Alone.* In the organic heat of her continuous presence he could not help but become interested once more in his muscles, his arteries, and nerve connections. In fact he began to love them, treasure them, praise them with funny little songs in *Man Does Live . . .*

> *the fingers of my flesh transcend*
> *my transcendental soul*
> *the tightness in my shoulders end*
> *my teeth have made me whole*

To the mouth of his head (that glory of will and determination) he brought hard apples, nuts, wheat germ, and soybean oil. He said to his old friends, From now on, I guess I'll keep my wits about me. I'm going on the natch. He said he was about to begin a spiritual deep-breathing journey. How about you too, Mom? he asked kindly.

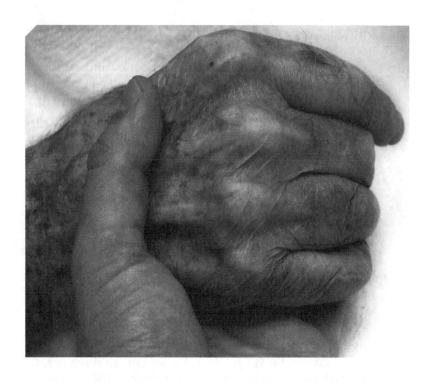

165   His conversion was so radiant, splendid, that neighborhood kids his age began to say that he had never been a real addict at all, only a journalist along for the smell of the story. The mother tried several times to give up what had become without her son and his
170 friends a lonely habit. This effort only brought it to supportable levels. The boy and his girl took their electronic mimeograph and moved to the bushy edge of another borough. They were very strict. They said they would not see her again until she had been off drugs for
175 sixty days.

    At home alone in the evening, weeping, the mother read and reread the seven issues of *Oh! Golden Horse!* They seemed to her as truthful as ever. We often crossed the street to visit and console. But if we mentioned any
180 of our children who were at college or in the hospital or dropouts at home, she would cry out, "My baby! My baby!" and burst into terrible, face-scarring, time-consuming tears. The End.

First my father was silent, then he said, "Number One: You have a nice sense of humor. Number Two: I see you can't tell a plain story. So don't waste time." Then he said sadly, "Number Three: I suppose that means she was alone, she was left like that, his mother. Alone. Probably sick?"

I said, "Yes."

"Poor woman. Poor girl, to be born in a time of **fools**, to live among fools. The end. The end. You were right to put that down. The end."

I didn't want to argue, but I had to say, "Well, it is not necessarily the end, Pa."

"Yes," he said, "what a tragedy. The end of a person."

"No, Pa," I begged him. "It doesn't have to be. She's only about forty. She could be a hundred different things in this world as time goes on. A teacher or a social worker. An ex-junkie! Sometimes it's better than having a master's in education."

"Jokes," he said. "As a writer that's your main trouble. You don't want to recognize it. Tragedy! Plain tragedy! Historical tragedy! No hope. The end."

"Oh, Pa," I said. "She could change."

"In your own life too, you have to look it in the face." He took a couple of nitroglycerin. "Turn to five," he said, pointing to the dial on the oxygen tank. He inserted the tubes into his nostrils and breathed deep. He closed his eyes and said, "No."

I had promised the family to always let him have the last word when arguing, but in this case I had a different responsibility. That woman lives across the street. She's my knowledge and my invention. I'm sorry for her. I'm not going to leave her there in that house crying. (Actually neither would Life, which unlike me has no pity.)

Therefore: She did change. Of course her son never came home again. But right now she's the receptionist in a storefront community clinic in the East Village. Most of the customers are young people, some old friends. The head doctor has said to her, "If we only had three people in this clinic with your experiences . . ."

"The doctor said that?" My father took the oxygen
225 tubes out of his nostrils and said, "Jokes. Jokes again."

"No, Pa, it could really happen that way, it's a funny
world nowadays."

"No," he said. "Truth first. She will slide back. A person
must have character. She does not."

230 "No, Pa," I said. "That's it. She's got a job. Forget it.
She's in that storefront working."

"How long will it be?" he asked. "Tragedy! You too.
When will you look it in the face?"

After Reading

1. What is the narrator's reaction to the father's request?

2. Where did the narrator get the idea for the story about the mother and son?

3. Why does the father reject his child's first attempt at the story?

4. What two jobs did the father hold during his lifetime? Do you think this is an unusual combination? Explain your answer.

5. Is the father satisfied with the narrator's second attempt at the story? Why or why not?

6. Why does the narrator refuse to accept that the story ends with the mother left alone?

7. Which of the two endings do you prefer: the ending in which the mother is left alone to read issues of *Oh! Golden Horse!* and grieve her loss **or** the suggested ending in which the mother finds a job as a receptionist in a community clinic? Explain your answer.

8. The narrator promised the family to always let the father have the last word when arguing. Does the father really have the last word in this story?

9. The story ends when the father says, "Tragedy! You too. When will you look it in the face?" What does he mean? To what is he referring?

10. Why do you think the father asks his child to write the story? Explain your answer.

Beyond the Lines

11. What do you think the author means when she writes, "Everyone, real or invented, deserves the open destiny of life"? Do you agree or disagree with this statement? Explain your answer.

12. The narrator always looks for the happy ending in stories. The father believes that his child is unable to recognize tragedy and look it in the face. Do you think that being hopeful and keeping a positive attitude is not realistic?

13. If you were to write a short story entitled "A Conversation With My Father," what would the content of your story be?

Guy de Maupassant (1850–1893) was born in Normandy, France, and spent his childhood there with his mother, He travelled extensively, and although he made many friends in literary circles, he preferred solitude. He was passionate about creating clever plot twists in his stories, as exemplified in "La Parure" ("The Diamond Necklace"), and he also wrote many stories in the fantasy genre, such as "Le Horla." In his later years, he developed a constant need to be alone, and became paranoid, most likely as a side effect of the syphilis he contracted in his early years. He was committed to an asylum in Paris after attempting suicide, and died there in 1893.

Before Reading

1. Read the words in the box below. Make sure you know the meaning of each one.

> shabby, knee breeches, soiled, gown, frock, coquettish, muttering, stammered, overwhelmed, priceless, dainty, frowsy, in despair, uttered, thunderstruck

Using the words in the box, find:
- Three words that describe how someone feels
- Three words that refer to what someone wears
- Three words associated with a luxurious lifestyle
- Three synonyms for the verb *speak*
- Three words associated with a lower-class lifestyle

2. Have you ever borrowed something from someone and lost it or damaged it? Has someone ever borrowed something from you and lost it or damaged it? Explain your answer.

3. The story "The Diamond Necklace" is set in Paris and was written in the late 19th century. What do you know about life during this era? Think about male and female roles as well as the differences in social classes.

While Reading

4. Pay attention to the descriptions of the life Mathilde actually lives and the life she desires. Write down information about the places she visits/would visit, the food she eats/would eat, the activities she does/would do, etc.

The Diamond Necklace

by Guy de Maupassant

T he girl was one of those pretty and charming young
creatures who sometimes are born, as if by a slip of
fate, into a family of clerks. She had no dowry, no
expectations, no way of being known, understood, loved,
5 married by any rich and distinguished man; so she let
herself be married to a little clerk of the Ministry of Public
Instruction.

She dressed plainly because she could not dress well,
but she was unhappy as if she had really fallen from a
10 higher station; since with women there is neither caste nor
rank, for beauty, grace and charm take the place of family
and birth. Natural ingenuity, instinct for what is elegant, a
supple mind are their sole hierarchy, and often make of
women of the people the equals of the very greatest ladies.

15 Mathilde suffered ceaselessly, feeling herself born to
enjoy all delicacies and all luxuries. She was distressed at
the poverty of her dwelling, at the bareness of the walls, at
the shabby chairs, the ugliness of the curtains. All those
things, of which another woman of her rank would never
20 even have been conscious, tortured her and made her
angry. The sight of the little Breton peasant who did her

humble housework aroused in her despairing regrets and bewildering dreams. She thought of silent antechambers hung with Oriental tapestry, illumined by tall bronze
25 candelabra, and of two great footmen in knee breeches who sleep in the big armchairs, made drowsy by the oppressive heat of the stove. She thought of long reception halls hung with ancient silk, of the dainty cabinets containing priceless curiosities and of the little coquettish perfumed reception
30 rooms made for chatting at five o'clock with intimate friends, with men famous and sought after, whom all women envy and whose attention they all desire.

When she sat down to dinner, before the round table covered with a tablecloth in use three days, opposite her
35 husband, who uncovered the soup **tureen** and declared with a delighted air, "Ah, the good soup! I don't know anything better than that," she thought of dainty dinners, of shining silverware, of tapestry that peopled the walls with ancient personages and with strange birds flying in the midst
40 of a fairy forest; and she thought of delicious dishes served on marvellous plates and of the whispered **gallantries** to which you listen with a sphinx-like smile while you are eating the pink meat of a trout or the wings of a quail.

She had no gowns, no jewels, nothing. And she loved
45 nothing but that. She felt made for that. She would have liked so much to please, to be envied, to be charming, to be sought after.

She had a friend, a former schoolmate at the convent, who was rich, and whom she did not like to go to see any
50 more because she felt so sad when she came home.

But one evening her husband reached home with a triumphant air and holding a large envelope in his hand.

"There," said he, "there is something for you."

She tore the paper quickly and drew out a printed card
55 which bore these words:

The Minister of Public Instruction and Madame Georges Ramponneau request the honor of M. and Madame Loisel's company at the palace of the Ministry on Monday evening, January 18th.

60 Instead of being delighted, as her husband had hoped, she threw the invitation on the table crossly, muttering:

"What do you wish me to do with that?"

"Why, my dear, I thought you would be glad. You never go out, and this is such a fine opportunity. I had great trouble to get it. Every one wants to go; it is very select, and they are not giving many invitations to clerks. The whole official world will be there."

She looked at him with an irritated glance and said impatiently: "And what do you wish me to put on my back?" He had not thought of that. He stammered: "Why, the gown you go to the theatre in. It looks very well to me." He stopped, distracted, seeing that his wife was weeping. Two great tears ran slowly from the corners of her eyes toward the corners of her mouth. "What's the matter? What's the matter?" he answered. By a violent effort she conquered her grief and replied in a calm voice, while she wiped her wet cheeks: "Nothing. Only I have no gown, and, therefore, I can't go to this ball. Give your card to some colleague whose wife is better equipped than I am."

He was in despair. He resumed:

"Come, let us see, Mathilde. How much would it cost, a suitable gown, which you could use on other occasions—something very simple?" She reflected several seconds, making her calculations and wondering also what sum she could ask without drawing on herself an immediate refusal and a frightened exclamation from the economical clerk. Finally she replied, hesitating:

"I don't know exactly, but I think I could manage it with four hundred francs." He grew a little pale, because he was laying aside just that amount to buy a gun and treat himself to a little shooting next summer on the plain of Nanterre, with several friends who went to shoot **larks** there on Sundays.

But he said:

"Very well. I will give you four hundred francs. And try to have a pretty gown." The day of the ball drew near and Madame Loisel seemed sad, uneasy, anxious. Her frock was ready, however. Her husband said to her one evening: "What is the matter? Come, you have

105 seemed very odd these last three days."

And she answered:

"It annoys me not to have a single piece of jewellery, not

110 a single ornament, nothing to put on. I shall look **poverty-stricken**. I would almost rather not go at all."

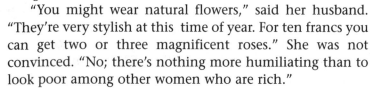

"You might wear natural flowers," said her husband.

115 "They're very stylish at this time of year. For ten francs you can get two or three magnificent roses." She was not convinced. "No; there's nothing more humiliating than to look poor among other women who are rich."

"How stupid you are!" her husband cried. "Go look up

120 your friend, Madame Forestier, and ask her to lend you some jewels. You're intimate enough with her to do that."

She uttered a cry of joy:

"True! I never thought of it."

The next day she went to her friend and told her of her

125 distress. Madame Forestier went to a wardrobe with a mirror, took out a large jewel box, brought it back, opened it and said to Madame Loisel:

"Choose, my dear."

She saw first some bracelets, then a pearl necklace, then

130 a Venetian gold cross set with precious stones, of admirable workmanship. She tried on the ornaments before the mirror, hesitated and could not make up her mind to part with them, to give them back. She kept asking:

"Haven't you any more?"

135 "Why, yes. Look further; I don't know what you like."

Suddenly she discovered, in a black satin box, a superb diamond necklace, and her heart **throbbed** with an immoderate desire. Her hands trembled as she took it. She **fastened** it round her throat, outside her high-necked

140 waist, and was lost in ecstasy at her reflection in the mirror.

Then she asked, hesitating, filled with anxious doubt:

"Will you lend me this, only this?"

"Why, yes, certainly."

She threw her arms round her friend's neck, kissed her
145 passionately, then fled with her treasure.

The night of the ball arrived. Madame Loisel was a great success. She was prettier than any other woman present, elegant, graceful, smiling and wild with joy. All the men looked at her, asked her name, sought to be introduced. All
150 the attachés of the Cabinet wished to waltz with her. She was remarked by the minister himself.

She danced with rapture, with passion, intoxicated by pleasure, forgetting all in the triumph of her beauty, in the glory of her success, in a sort of cloud of happiness
155 comprised of all this homage, admiration, these awakened desires and of that sense of triumph which is so sweet to a woman's heart.

She left the ball about four o'clock in the morning. Her husband had been sleeping since midnight in a little
160 deserted back room alongside three other gentlemen whose wives were enjoying the ball.

He threw over her shoulders the wraps he had brought, the modest wraps of common life, the poverty of which contrasted with the elegance of the ball dress. She felt this
165 and wished to escape so as not to be remarked by the other women, who were enveloping themselves in costly furs.

Loisel held her back, saying: "Wait a bit. You will catch cold outside. I will call a cab."

But she did not listen to him and rapidly descended the
170 stairs. When they reached the street they could not find a carriage and began to look for one, shouting after the cabmen passing at a distance.

They went toward the Seine in despair, shivering with cold. At last they found on the quay one of those ancient
175 night cabs which, as though they were ashamed to show their shabbiness during the day, are never seen around Paris until after dark.

180 It took them to their dwelling in the Rue des Martyrs, and sadly

they mounted the stairs to their flat. All was ended for her. As to him, he reflected that he must be at the ministry at ten o'clock that morning.

185 She removed her wraps before the glass so as to see herself once more in all her glory. But suddenly she uttered a cry. She no longer had the necklace around her neck!

"What is the matter with you?" demanded her husband, already half undressed.

190 She turned distractedly toward him.

"I have—I have—I've lost Madame Forestier's necklace," she cried.

He stood up, bewildered.

"What!—how? Impossible!"

195 They looked among the folds of her skirt, of her cloak, in her pockets, everywhere, but did not find it.

"You're sure you had it on when you left the ball?" he asked.

"Yes, I felt it in the vestibule of the minister's house."

200 "But if you had lost it in the street we should have heard it fall. It must be in the cab."

"Yes, probably. Did you take his number?"

"No. And you—didn't you notice it?"

"No."

205 They looked, thunderstruck, at each other. At last Loisel put on his clothes.

"I shall go back on foot," said he, "over the whole route, to see whether I can find it."

He went out. She sat waiting on a chair in her ball dress,
210 without strength to go to bed, overwhelmed, without any fire, without a thought. Her husband returned about seven o'clock. He had found nothing.

He went to police headquarters, to the newspaper offices to offer a reward; he went to the cab companies—
215 everywhere, in fact, where he was urged by the least spark of hope.

She waited all day, in the same condition of mad fear before this terrible calamity.

Loisel returned at night with a hollow, pale face. He had
220 discovered nothing.

"You must write to your friend," said he, "that you have broken the clasp of her necklace and that you are having it mended. That will give us time to turn around."

She wrote at his dictation.

225 At the end of a week they had lost all hope. Loisel, who had aged five years, declared:

"We must consider how to replace that ornament."

The next day they took the box that had contained it and went to the jeweller whose name was found within. He 230 consulted his books.

"It was not I, Madame, who sold that necklace; I must simply have furnished the case."

Then they went from jeweller to jeweller, searching for a necklace like the other, trying to recall it, both sick with 235 chagrin and grief.

They found, in a shop at the Palais Royal, a string of diamonds that seemed to them exactly like the one they had lost. It was worth forty thousand francs. They could have it for thirty-six.

240 So they begged the jeweller not to sell it for three days yet. And they made a **bargain** that he should buy it back for thirty-four thousand francs, in case they should find the lost necklace before the end of February.

Loisel possessed eighteen thousand francs which his 245 father had left him. He would borrow the rest.

He did borrow, asking a thousand francs of one, five hundred of another, five louis here, three louis there. He gave notes, took up ruinous obligations, dealt with **usurers** and all the race of lenders. He compromised all 250 the rest of his life, risked signing a note without even knowing whether he could meet it; and, frightened by the trouble yet to come, by the black misery that was about to fall upon him, by the prospect of all the physical 255 privations and moral tortures that he was to suffer, he went to get the new necklace, laying upon the jeweller's counter thirty-six thousand francs.

VOCABULARY
bargain: an agreement between two parties
usurer: a person who lends money and charges interest

²⁶⁰ When Madame Loisel took back the necklace Madame Forestier said to her with a chilly manner:

"You should have returned it sooner; I might have needed it."

She did not open the case, as her friend had so much ²⁶⁵ feared. If she had detected the substitution, what would she have thought, what would she have said? Would she not have taken Madame Loisel for a thief?

Thereafter Madame Loisel knew the horrible existence of the needy. She bore her part, however, with sudden ²⁷⁰ heroism. That dreadful debt must be paid. She would pay it. They dismissed their servant; they changed their lodgings; they rented a **garret** under the roof.

She came to know what heavy housework meant and the **odious** cares of the kitchen. She washed the dishes, ²⁷⁵ using her dainty fingers and rosy nails on greasy pots and pans. She washed the soiled linen, the shirts and the dishcloths, which she dried upon a line; she carried the slops down to the street every morning and carried up the water, stopping for breath at every landing. And dressed ²⁸⁰ like a woman of the people, she went to the fruiterer, the grocer, the butcher, a basket on her arm, bargaining, meeting with impertinence, defending her miserable money, sou by sou.

Every month they had to meet some notes, renew
285 others, obtain more time. Her husband worked evenings,
making up a tradesman's accounts, and late at night he
often copied manuscript for five sous a page.

This life lasted ten years.

At the end of ten years they had paid everything,
290 everything, with the rates of usury and the accumulations
of the compound interest.

Madame Loisel looked old now. She had become the
woman of impoverished households—strong and hard and
rough. With frowsy hair, skirts **askew** and red hands, she
295 talked loud while washing the floor with great swishes of
water. But sometimes, when her husband was at the office,
she sat down near the window and she thought of that gay
evening of long ago, of that ball where she had been so
beautiful and so admired.

300 What would have happened if she had not lost that
necklace? Who knows? who knows? How strange and
changeful is life! How small a thing can be to make or
ruin us!

But one Sunday, having gone to take a walk in the
305 Champs-Elysées to refresh herself after the labours of the
week, she suddenly perceived a woman who was leading a
child. It was Madame Forestier, still young, still beautiful,
still charming.

Madame Loisel felt moved. Should she speak to her?
310 Yes, certainly. And now that she had paid, she would tell
her all about it. Why not?

She went up.

"Good-day, Jeanne."

The other, astonished to be familiarly addressed by
315 this plain housewife, did not recognize her at all and
stammered:

"But—Madame!—I do not
know—You must be mistaken."

"No. I am Mathilde Loisel."

320 Her friend uttered a cry.

"Oh, my poor Mathilde!
How you have changed!"

"Yes, I have had a pretty hard life, since I last saw you, and great poverty—and that because of you!"

325 "Of me! How so?"

"Do you remember that diamond necklace you lent me to wear at the ministerial ball?"

"Yes. Well?"

"Well, I lost it."

330 "What do you mean? You brought it back."

"I brought you back another exactly like it. And it has taken us ten years to pay for it. You can understand that it was not easy for us, for us who had nothing. At last it is ended, and I am very glad."

335 Madame Forestier had stopped.

"You say that you bought a necklace of diamonds to replace mine?"

"Yes. You never noticed it, then! They were very similar."

340 And she smiled with a joy that was at once proud and ingenuous.

Madame Forestier, deeply moved, took her hands.

"Oh, my poor Mathilde! Why, the jewels in my necklace were made of paste! It was worth at most only five
345 hundred francs!"

After Reading

1. Why was Mathilde so dissatisified with her lot in life?

2. Describe the relationship between Mathilde and her husband.

3. Why did Mathilde no longer visit her schoolmate from the convent?

4. Why is Mathilde angry about the invitation to the Ministry event and why is her husband surprised by her reaction?

5. Describe Mathilde's experience at the ball.

6. What reason does Mathilde's husband suggest for not returning the necklace right away?

7. How did the Loisels manage to raise the 36 000 francs?

8. What was Madame Forestier's reaction when Mathilde returned the necklace?

9. How long did it take the Loisels to reimburse the loan?

10. The author, Guy De Maupassant, was known for creating clever plot twists in his stories. What is the plot twist in "The Diamond Necklace?" Did the ending of the story surprise you? Why or why not? Was there any clue as to the value of the diamond necklace earlier on in the story?

11. Why do you think Madame Forestier never contacted Mathilde after the return of her necklace?

12. Continue the conversation between Madame Forestier and Mathilde.

Beyond the Lines

13. Mathilde sometimes thought of the evening many years before when she enjoyed her time in the spotlight. She thinks of the necklace and how it changed her life. The author writes, "How strange and changeful is life! How small a thing can be to make or ruin us!" Was it really the diamond necklace that changed the course of Mathilde's life? Do you think Mathilde would choose to live those ten years again for the night of glory she experienced at the ball?

14. Do you think Mathilde did the right thing by telling Madame Forestier the truth about the necklace so many years later?

15. How do you think M. Loisel will react to the news? Do you think Mathilde will tell him? Do you think she should tell him?

16. Honesty is the best policy. Do you think this proverb applies in this story? Use information from the text to support your answer.

Born in 1974, Carrie Haber is a writer, filmmaker and musician from Montréal, Québec. She plays cello and electroacoustic instruments in her one-woman show, Solo&Inch, and composes music for film and radio. She also has written a show for CBC Radio about the influence of current affairs on children, and devotes much of her time to working with community organizations. Her stories have appeared in several literary journals and anthologies.

Before Reading

1. Find and write the definition of each of the words below. Then, use each word in a sentence.

   a) bale   **b)** barn   **c)** landscape   **d)** quilt   **e)** tweed

2. Read the title of the story. Using the title for ideas as well as the words in question 1, what do you think the story will be about?

3. Have you ever been to a fair? What types of activities are usually offered at a fair? What sort of rides are there? Describe the atmosphere.

4. Have you, or has someone you know ever taken a ride in a hot air balloon? What do you think it would be like? Is this something that you would like to experience? Explain your answer.

While Reading

5. Mood is the atmosphere or climate created in a story. It is created by the author's choice of language, as well as the characters, setting and events in the story. What mood is created in the introduction to this story?

6. How does the author create the mood of the story?

7. Pay attention to the setting of the story. How does the author's choice of setting contrast the mood of the story?

8. List ten new words or expressions you learned while reading the story.

"The Unsanded Balloon"

by Carrie Haber

T he sky was a cross between film grain and toothpaste, and it made all the cows in the landscape tingle with a quiet knowledge of what was coming.

The bluegrass stage in the main barn was enclosed by a
5 semicircle of old-timers, bent this way, crooked that way, in suspenders, tweed, crisp jeans, and flatflower dresses.

Children tumbled, tagged and fought in the bales by the corner. Everyone else sat, stood, danced, drank, and talked about this year's crops, and this and that. Women
10 were lined up along the back wall, raffling off thick, dry cookies, a quilt, and at least twelve sets of somewhat inspired salt-and-pepper shakers.

Outside, Wilson was flaming up his hot-air balloon for two-ticket rides. He stood in his basket, cranked his neck,
15 and allowed himself the superb dizziness of this position, watching the fluttering silk rise. His jeans hung loosely, as did his face, giving him the stature of an old pelican that has just swallowed too big a catch. A few children had gathered to watch, and he ignored them.
20 "How far can it go, mister?"

"How *high* can it go?"

"Can we have a ride?"

"I was here *first*."

Wilson gazed into his inflating dome, as though
25 helpless in prayer under a chapel fresco. The flame's roar
hurt his ears, and the gas and heat and rush turned
everything he saw to liquid. The ground below was sopping
with soda and **livestock** urine. A baby goat chewed the leg
of the picnic table it was tied to. It paused to watch the
30 various creatures scramble in the nearby pen: five-dollar
rabbits, an oily black sheep and her offspring, adamant
ducks. A sore cow, who just lay near her latest excrement in
a **sullen torpor**, heavily blinked and chewed on
something the children had passed her.

35 One of Wilson's little girls sat on a bench near the barn
door, her pink T-shirt proud along the **collarbone** with
prize ribbons. She hadn't looked at any other children after
winning the three-legged race and popcorn-stringing
contest and avoided stares as she walked away from the
40 dunking booth where she'd successfully sunk her brother.
She was famous that day, and it burned. The other
children's gazes were spiked with heat; a few of the little

rrie Haber

ones had followed her from contest to contest and stood beside her as she lined up for candy. She'd heard them whisper when she passed them. Now she sat by herself in the barn, half in broken sunlight, half in the **musty** shadow of the barn beams. Her legs were covered in fine blond hair, mosquito bites, and scrapes. She cupped three bunnies on her lap, **deflecting** their every effort to jump down with her rigid, careful palms. Through the open barn door she could see her father, a ripe strawberry bulging from his basket, and did not expect him to look back. She wanted to say, "Here I am, Daddy." Or, "Look how good I am with the rabbits." Or, "Look at this poor old cow."

Wilson felt small movements all around him. Corn popping. Fifty cents being spent on things. Cigarettes being passed around by young people in bad haircuts, shivering under three or four raindrops. The thin glimmer of **pinwheels** under a bright grey sky. It was all the regular patter of every year's fair. Wilson could not remember it ever being different, except last year, when they invited Carla Farnham, the country singer. Everyone had been sure to be inside the barn for her afternoon performance, including Wilson, but, when Carla came in the wrong door and pushed through the crowd with her guitar case, she turned out to be fat and ended up playing bad rock covers in a featherlight strum. Today, Wilson caught the little sounds and movements around him and collected them in that hobo's kerchief part of the brain that packs these things lightly before a voyage. He imagined himself a few other people—an Italian **seafarer**, for example, preparing his craft with his back to the sounds of the port, the fishermen **haggling** with merchants, the

VOCABULARY

collarbone: clavicle

deflecting: turning aside or heading off

haggling: bargaining

livestock: animals kept on a farm, such as horses, cows and sheep

musty: to have an odour of mould

pinwheel: a type of firework

seafarer: a sailor

sullen: irritated and gloomy

torpor: a state of indifference or inactivity

dockworkers talking sports. The balloon slowly filled. The children that had lined up were given rides, while Wilson
85 watched the horizons on all sides rise and fall, rise and fall.

At the other side of the fairground, there was Burton.

Burton was the kid who threw up in the trashcan behind the hot dog booth, and everybody saw—and anybody who didn't see, heard. A few families, cluttered around the
90 picnic tables that stuck out from under the plastic canopy, were the first to see Burton standing lonely beside the trash can, like a well-trained dog caught in too many scents and not knowing which way to go. The can came up to his shoulders, and his hair was in his eyes. There was heat
95 coming off that boy, and, if it wasn't from crying, it was from the throbs of embarrassment that wracked his little frame. There was no running water on the grounds, and Burton felt trapped under the heavy **stench** of his insides, in front of the whole town. He could see his parents' barn
100 atop a far hill, ten kilometres away. He started to run for the barn, and then, like a spooked horse, changed his mind. He turned and ran right through the crowd, between the booths and the barn, and his lungs hurt.

arrie Haber

Past the fairground, there was nothing but the centre of town, where the park was. The park, this time of day, was full of grade eights from his class.

Wilson was on his way up, **teetering** with the weight of the sandbags he had not yet thrown overboard. The slow and gargantuan balloon—with its red and yellow bulges against the grey, drizzling air—was a beacon of content. It was a balloon. It was nothing to be ashamed of. It told Burton so. Burton ran for Wilson and stopped at the rope-hold.

"You're too big, kid." Wilson slumped a sandbag up onto the side of the basket and told Burton to get out of the way. Burton reached up and pulled the sandbag to the ground. Wilson **heaved** another.

"Watch yer fingers, kid."

"I'm thir*teen*." Burton was reasoning with his left foot, as it took hold in a divet on the basket. He was not convincing Wilson of much, who clearly did not want the company. One sandbag left. Wilson kept an eye on the frantic boy, who was hyperventilating as he tried to climb into the basket.

"You got ears or no? This is going up—move it."

Burton struggled to **clamber** into the basket the way a waterlogged dog struggles to climb onto a raft. He had no ears, not eyes, not any sense except pure, cold, wholly consuming fear. He grabbed a rope and pulled himself up onto the basket ledge.

Wilson put his hands against the boy and pushed, and Burton fell to the ground with all the ceremony of the last sandbag. Wilson thrust a long flame into the balloon and began to rise, watching the people stream towards the still boy, and did not shout back. The flame hushed out the crowd's raging. Wilson turned to face the mountains—the dark, **prone** chain distilled into

VOCABULARY

clamber: climb with difficulty

heaved: lifted with effort and force

prone: sloping or in a downward direction

stench: an offensive odour

teetering: moving in an unsteady way

the landscape. He became smaller and smaller as he floated
145 over them, over cows, and over any **remnant** wanting.
He floated, and the floating inhaled him like all the other
clouds.

Wilson's little girl did not watch her father disappear
any longer. She stayed inside the barn for a long time,
150 whispering promises to the rabbits.

After Reading

1. Respond to the text using **three** of the prompts below.

   - *I enjoyed/didn't enjoy this story because . . .*
   - *I found it difficult to understand . . .*
   - *The character I found the most interesting is . . . because . . .*
   - *I had a similar experience when . . .*
   - *I think the author's message is . . .*

2. List the activities offered at this year's fair.

3. What type of child is Wilson's little girl? Support your answer with information from the text.

4. Describe the relationship between Wilson and his daughter.

5. How do you think Wilson would describe the fair?

6. How had the special guest at the previous year's fair turned out to be a disappointment?

7. What do you think the author means when she writes, "Today, Wilson caught the little sounds and movements around him and collected them in that hobo's kerchief part of the brain that packs these things lightly before a voyage"?

8. Who does Wilson imagine himself to be?

9. Who is Burton? What do you think his role is in the story? Use information from the text to support your ideas.

10. Why do you think Burton wanted to get into the basket so badly?

11. What promises do you think Wilson's daughter might be whispering to the rabbits?

12. Did the ending of the story surprise you? What clues does the author give as to how the story might end?

Beyond the Lines

13. What impact will the events in the story have on next year's fair?

14. What message do you think the author wants to share with her readers?

Laurie Halse Anderson, an American writer of children's and young adult fiction, was born in Potsdam, New York, in 1961. After high school, she spent time working on a farm in Denmark, and then returned to the United States to attend a community college. She later transferred to Georgetown University, where she earned a degree in Languages and Linguistics. *Speak* is her first and most famous novel, released in 1999, and she has since written several award-winning novels for young adults, including the novel *Twisted,* and has written two volumes of a historical fiction narrative series entitled *Chains.*

Before Reading

1. The author of the story uses informal language and slang typically used by teens. Rewrite the following sentences replacing the words in italics with more formal language.

   a) Mr. Neck changed it at the very last second because he wants *to flunk me* or hates me or something.

   b) I'm not going to let an idiot teacher *jerk me around* like this.

   c) I showed up every day this semester, *sat my butt* in every class, did some homework, and didn't cheat on tests.

   d) I still *get slammed in* MISS.

   e) So why does everyone *make such a big hairy deal* about me not talking?

   f) "Do you lecture all your friends like this?" "Only the ones I like." We both *chew on this* for a minute.

2. Make a list of problems that teenagers commonly face during their high school years. Which of these problems do you think teenagers find difficult to talk about?

While Reading

3. Pay attention to descriptions of the main character, Melinda. Write down information about her thoughts, speech, actions and feelings as she faces various conflicts in the story.

4. Summarize in one sentence the main idea of each of the sections: No Justice, No Peace; Advice from a Smart Mouth; The Beast Prowls.

From *Speak*

by Laurie Halse Anderson

NO JUSTICE, NO PEACE

There is no way I'm reading my **suffragette** report in front of the class. That wasn't part of the original
5 assignment. Mr. Neck changed it at the very last second because he wants to flunk me or hates me or something. But I've written a really good report and I'm not going to let an idiot teacher jerk me around like this. I ask David Petrakis for advice. We come up with a Plan.

10   I get to class early, when Mr. Neck is still in the lounge. I write what I need to on the board and cover the words with a suffragette protest sign. My box from the copy shop is on the floor. Mr. Neck walks in. He grumbles that I can go first. I stand suffragette tall and calm. It is a lie. My
15 insides feel like I'm caught in a tornado. My toes curl inside my sneakers, trying to grip the floor so I won't get sucked out the window.

     Mr. Neck nods at me. I pick
20 up my report as if I'm going to read it out loud. I stand there,

VOCABULARY

suffragette: a woman who fought for women's right to vote papers trembling as if a breeze is blowing through the closed door. I turn around and rip my poster off the blackboard.

THE SUFFRAGETTES FOUGHT FOR THE RIGHT TO SPEAK.

25 THEY WERE ATTACKED, ARRESTED, AND THROWN IN JAIL FOR DARING TO DO WHAT THEY WANTED. LIKE THEY WERE, I AM WILLING TO STAND UP FOR WHAT I BELIEVE. NO ONE SHOULD BE FORCED TO GIVE SPEECHES. I CHOOSE TO STAY SILENT.

The class reads slowly, some of them moving their lips.
30 Mr. Neck turns around to see what everyone is staring at. I nod at David. He joins me at the front of the room and I hand him my box.

David: "Melinda has to deliver her report to the class as part of the assignment. She made copies everyone can read."

35 He passes out the copies. They cost me $6.72 at the office supply store. I was going to make a cover page and color it, but I haven't gotten much **allowance** recently, so I just put the title at the top of the first page.

My plan is to stand in front of the class for the five
40 minutes I was given for my presentation. The suffragettes must have planned out and timed their protests, too. Mr. Neck has other plans. He gives me a D and escorts me to the authorities. I forgot about how the suffragettes were hauled off to jail. Duh. I go on a tour of the guidance
45 counselor's office, Principal Principal's, and wind up back in MISS, I am back to being a Discipline Problem again.

I need a lawyer. I showed up every day this semester, sat my butt in every class, did some homework, and didn't cheat on tests. I still get slammed in MISS. There is no way
50 they can punish me for not speaking. It isn't fair. What do they know about me? What do they know about the inside of my head? Flashes of lightning, children crying. Caught in an avalanche, pinned by worry, **squirming** under the weight of doubt, guilt. Fear.

55 The walls in MISS are still white. Andy Beast isn't here. Thank God for small favors. A boy with lime-colored hair who looks like he's channeling for an alien species **dozes**; two goths in black velvet dresses and artfully torn pantyhose trade Mona Lisa smiles. They cut school to stand
60 in line for killer concert tickets. MISS is a small price to pay for Row 10, seats 21 and 22.

I **simmer**. Lawyers on TV always tell their clients not
to say anything. The cops say that thing: "Anything you
say will be used against you." Self-incrimination. I looked it
65 up. Three-point vocab word. So why does everyone make
such a big hairy deal about me not talking? Maybe I don't
want to incriminate myself. Maybe I don't like the sound of
my voice. Maybe I don't have anything to say.

The boy with the lime-colored hair wakes up when he
70 falls out of his chair. The Gothgirls whinny. Mr. Neck picks
his nose when he thinks we aren't looking. I need a lawyer.

ADVICE FROM A SMART MOUTH

75 David Petrakis sends me a
note in social studies. Typed.
He thinks it's horrible that
my parents didn't videotape
Mr. Neck's class or stick up
80 for me the way his folks did.
It feels so good to have
someone feel sorry for me,
I don't mention that my
parents don't know what
85 happened. They'll figure
out what happened soon
enough at the next meeting
with the guidance counselor.

I think David should be a judge. His latest career goal
90 is to be a quantum-physics genius. I don't know what
that means, but he says his father is furious. His dad is
right—David was made for the
law: deadly calm, turbo-charged
brain, and a good eye for
95 weakness.

He stops by my locker. I tell
him Mr. Neck gave me a D for
the suffragette report.

David: "He has a point."

100 Me: "It was a great report!
You read it. I wrote a bibliography

VOCABULARY

allowance: a sum
of money given to
children by parents
dozes: sleeps lightly
simmer: remain quiet
in a state of anger
squirming: wriggling

and I didn't copy from the encyclopedia. It was the best report ever. It's not my fault Mr. Neck doesn't get performance art."

105 David pauses to offer me a stick of gum. It's a delaying tactic, the kind that juries love.

David: "But you got it wrong. The suffragettes were all about speaking up, screaming for their rights. You can't speak up for your right to be silent. That's letting the bad

110 guys win. If the suffragettes did that, women wouldn't be able to vote yet."

I blow a bubble in his face. He folds the gum wrappers into tiny triangles.

David: "Don't get me wrong. I think what you did was

115 kind of cool and getting stuck in MISS wasn't fair. But don't expect to make a difference unless you speak up for yourself."

Me: "Do you lecture all your friends like this?"

David: "Only the ones I like."

120 We both chew on this for a minute. The bell rings. I keep looking in my locker for a book that I already know isn't there. David checks his watch a hundred times. We hear Principal Principal **bellow**, "Let's move it, people!"

David: "Maybe I'll call you."

125 Me: "Maybe I won't answer." Chew, chew. Blowbubblepop. "Maybe I will."

Is he asking me out? I don't think so. But he kind of is. I guess I'll answer if he calls. But if he touches me I'll explode, so a date is out of the question. No touching.

130

THE BEAST PROWLS

I stay after school to work on tree sketches. Mr. Freeman helps me for a while. He gives me a roll of brown paper and

135 a piece of white chalk and shows me how to draw a tree in three sweeping lines. He doesn't care how many mistakes I make, just one-two-three, "like a waltz," he says. Over and over. I use up a mile of the paper, but he doesn't care. This may be the root of his budget problem with the school board.

140 God crackles over the intercom and tells Mr. Freeman he's late for a faculty meeting. Mr. Freeman says the kind of

words you don't usually hear from teachers. He gives me a new piece of chalk and tells me
145 to draw roots. You can't grow a decent tree without roots.

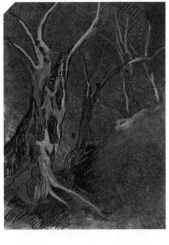

The art room is one of the places I feel safe. I hum and don't worry about looking
150 stupid. Roots. Ugh. But I try. One-two-three, one-two-three. I don't worry about the next day or minute. One-two-three.

Somebody flicks the lights
155 off. My head snaps up. IT is there. Andy Beast. Little rabbit heart leaps out of my chest and **scampers** across the paper, leaving bloody footprints on my roots. He turns the lights back on.

I smell him. Have to find out where he gets that
160 cologne. I think it's called Fear. This is turning into one of those repeating nightmares where you keep falling but never hit the floor. Only I feel like I just smacked into the ground at a hundred miles an hour.

IT: "You seen Rachelle? Rachelle Bruin?"
165 I sit completely still. Maybe I can blend in with the metal tables and crumbling clay pots. He walks toward me, long, slow strides. The smell chokes me. I shiver.

IT: "She's supposed to meet me, but I can't find her anywhere. You know who she is?"
170 Me:

IT sits on my table, ITs leg **smears** my chalk drawing, **blurring** the roots into a mossy fog.

175 IT: "Hello? Anyone home? Are you deaf?"

IT stares at my face. I crush my jaws together so hard my teeth crumble to dust.

180 I am a deer frozen in the headlights of a tractor trailer. Is

From *Speak* 81

he going to hurt me again? He couldn't, not in school. Could he? Why can't I scream, say something, do anything? Why am I so afraid?

185 "Andy? I've been waiting outside." Rachel sweeps into the room wearing an artsy-fartsy gypsy scarf skirt and a necklace of eye-sized mirrors. She pouts and Andy leaps off the table, ripping my paper, scattering bits of chalk. Ivy walks through the door, bumping Rachel accidentally. She
190 hesitates—she has to feel that something is going on—then she takes her sculpture off the shelf and sits at the table next to me. Rachel looks at me, but she doesn't say anything. She must have gotten my note—I mailed it over a week ago. I stand up. Rachel gives us a half wave and says
195 "Ciao." Andy puts his arm around her waist and pulls her close to his body as they float out the door.

Ivy is talking to me, but it takes a while before I can hear her. "What a jerk," she says. She pinches the clay. "I can't believe she's going out with him. Can you? It's like
200 I don't know her anymore. And he's trouble." She slaps a hunk of clay on the table. "Believe me, that creep is trouble with a capital T."

I'd love to stay and chat, but my feet won't let me. I walk home instead of taking the bus, I unlock the front
205 door and walk straight up to my room, across the rug, and into my closet without even taking off my backpack. When I close the closet door behind me, I bury my face into the clothes on the left side of the rack, clothes that haven't fit for years. I stuff my mouth with old fabric and scream until
210 there are no sounds left under my skin.

After Reading

1. What is ironic about Melinda's decision to remain silent during the presentation of her suffragette report?

2. What do you think about the Plan? Do you think Melinda did the right thing by refusing to speak?

3. Why does Melinda feel that her punishment at school is unfair?

4. Why does David agree with Mr. Neck's decision to give Melinda a D for her suffragette report?

5. Describe Melinda's friend, David. Is David a good friend to Melinda? Support your answer with information from the text.

6. Who is IT?

7. Describe Melinda's reaction when Andy Beast appears while she is working on her art project. Why do you think she reacts this way?

8. How is Andy's behaviour intimidating?

9. Do you think Beast is Andy's real surname? Explain your answer.

10. Melinda offers possible reasons why she doesn't talk. "Maybe I don't want to incriminate myself. Maybe I don't like the sound of my voice. Maybe I don't have anything to say." What do you think are the reasons for Melinda's silence?

11. David says, "But don't expect to make a difference unless you speak up for yourself." What significance does this statement hold for Melinda?

12. What are some examples of internal and external conflict that Melinda faces in the story?

Beyond the Lines

13. If Melinda decided to speak, what do you think she would say?

14. Have you ever been in a situation where you chose to stay silent even though you knew you should speak up about something?

15. What would you do if you learned that a friend of yours had been the perpetrator or the victim of sexual abuse?

Before Reading

1. Write the definition of each of the following verbs: blurt out; swagger; waver; fire; grope

   Complete the sentences with the verbs listed above. Remember to use the correct form of each verb.

   a) It is a very humiliating experience to be _____ from a job.

   b) The girl _____ in the bottom of her bag to find her keys.

   c) His voice _____ as he stepped up to address the audience.

   d) Tristan _____ into the ring, confident of his victory.

   e) Sarah always _____ the answer without thinking.

2. What is your definition of growing up? At what point in life do you think a youth becomes an adult?

3. Do you think parents should do everything they can to protect their children in any situation? Should parents always be held responsible for their children's acts? Explain your answer.

While Reading

4. How does Alfred's character develop through the events in the story?

5. Who is the stronger character, Sam Carr or Mrs. Higgins? Support your answer using information from the text.

All the Years of Her Life

by Morley Callaghan

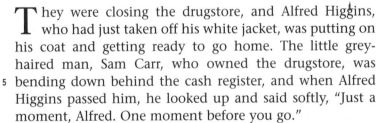

They were closing the drugstore, and Alfred Higgins, who had just taken off his white jacket, was putting on his coat and getting ready to go home. The little grey-haired man, Sam Carr, who owned the drugstore, was
5 bending down behind the cash register, and when Alfred Higgins passed him, he looked up and said softly, "Just a moment, Alfred. One moment before you go."

The soft, confident, and quiet way in which Sam Carr spoke made Alfred start to button his coat nervously. He
10 felt sure his face was white. Sam Carr usually said, "Good night," brusquely, without looking up. In the six months he had been working in the drugstore, Alfred had never heard his employer speak softly like that. His heart began to beat so loud it was hard for him to get his breath. "What
15 is it, Mr. Carr?" he asked.

"Maybe you'd be good enough to take a few things out of your pocket and leave them here before you go," Sam Carr said.

"What things? What are you talking about?"
20 "You've got a compact and a lipstick and at least two tubes of toothpaste in your pockets, Alfred."

"What do you mean? Do you think I'm crazy?" Alfred blustered. His face got red and he knew he looked fierce with indignation. But Sam Carr, standing by the door with
25 his blue eyes shining brightly behind his glasses and his lips moving underneath his grey moustache, only nodded his head a few times, and then Alfred grew very frightened and he didn't know what to say. Slowly he raised his hand and dipped it into his pocket, and with his eyes never
30 meeting Sam Carr's eyes, he took out the blue compact and the two tubes of toothpaste and a lipstick, and he laid them one by one on the counter.

"**Petty thieving**, eh, Alfred"! Sam Carr said. "And maybe you'd be good enough to tell me how long this has
35 been going on."

"This is the first time I ever took anything."

"So now you think you'll tell me a lie, eh? What kind of a **sap** do I look like, huh? I don't know what goes on in my own store, eh? I tell you you've been doing this pretty
40 steady," Sam Carr said as he went over and stood behind the cash register.

Ever since Alfred had left school he had been getting into trouble wherever he worked. He lived with his mother and his father, who was a printer. His two older brothers
45 were married and his sister had got married last year, and it would have been all right for his parents now if Alfred had only been able to keep a job.

While Sam Carr smiled and stroked the side of his face very delicately with the tips of his fingers, Alfred began to
50 feel that familiar terror growing in him that had been in him every time he had got into such trouble.

"I liked you," Sam Carr was saying. "I liked you and would have trusted you, and now look what I got to do."
While Alfred watched with his alert, frightened blue eyes,
55 Sam Carr drummed with his fingers on the counter. "I don't like to call a cop in **point-blank**," he was saying as he looked very worried. "You're a fool and maybe I should call your father and tell him you're a fool. Maybe I should let them know I'm going to have you locked up."

60 "My father's not at home. He's a printer. He works nights," Alfred said.

"Who's at home?"

"My mother, I guess."

"Then we'll see what she says." Sam Carr went to the
65 phone and dialed the number. Alfred was not so much
ashamed, but there was that deep fright growing in him,
and he blurted out arrogantly, like a strong, full-grown
man. "Just a minute. You don't need to draw anybody else
in. You don't need to tell her." He wanted to sound like a
70 swaggering, big guy who could look after himself, yet the
old, childish hope was in him, the longing that someone at
home would come and help him. "Yeah, that's right, he's in
trouble," Mr Carr was saying. "Yeah, your boy works for
me. You'd better come down in a hurry." And when he was
75 finished Mr Carr went over to the door and looked out at
the street and watched the people passing in the late
summer night. "I'll keep my eye out for a cop," was all he
said.

Alfred knew how his mother would come rushing in;
80 she would rush in with her eyes **blazing**, or maybe she
would be crying, and she would push him away when he
tried to talk to her, and make him feel her dreadful
contempt; yet he longed that she might come before Mr.
Carr saw the cop on the beat
85 passing the door.

While they waited—and it
seemed a long time—they did
not speak, and when at last they
heard someone tapping on the
90 closed door, Mr. Carr, turning
the **latch**, said crisply, "Come
in, Mrs. Higgins." He looked
hard-faced and stern.

Mrs. Higgins must have been
95 going to bed when he
telephoned, for her hair was
tucked in loosely under her hat,
and her hand at her throat held
her light coat tight across her
100 chest so her dress would not
show. She came in, large and

VOCABULARY

ashamed: embarrassed by feelings of guilt

blazing: burning brightly

contempt: extreme distaste for someone or something

latch: a device used to lock a door

petty: insignificant

point-blank: straightforward; directly

sap: a fool

thieving: stealing

plump, with a little smile on her friendly face. Most of the store lights had
105 been turned out and at first she did not see Alfred, who was standing in the shadow at the end of the counter. Yet as
110 soon as she saw him she did not look as Alfred thought she would look; she smiled, her blue eyes never wavered, and with
115 a calmness and dignity that made them forget that her clothes seemed

to have been thrown on her, she put out her hand to Mr. Carr and said politely, "I'm Mrs. Higgins. I'm Alfred's
120 mother."

Mr. Carr was a bit embarrassed by her lack of terror and her simplicity, and he hardly knew what to say to her, so she asked, "Is Alfred in trouble?"

"He is. He's been taking things from the store. I caught
125 him **red-handed**. Little things like compacts and toothpaste and lipsticks. Stuff he can sell easily," the proprietor said.

As she listened, Mrs. Higgins looked at Alfred sometimes and nodded her head sadly, and when Sam Carr
130 had finished she said gravely, "Is it so, Alfred?"

"Yes."

"Why have you been doing it?"

"I've been spending money, I guess."

"On what?"

135 "Going around with the guys, I guess," Alfred said.

Mrs. Higgins put out her hand and touched Sam Carr's arm with an understanding gentleness, and speaking as though afraid of disturbing him, she said, "If you would only listen to me before doing anything." Her simple
140 **earnestness** made her shy; her humility made her falter and look away, but in a moment she was smiling gravely

again, and she said with a kind of patient dignity, "What did you intend to do, Mr. Carr?"

"I was going to get a cop. That's what I ought to do."

145 "Yes, I suppose so. It's not for me to say, because he's my son. Yet I sometimes think a little good advice is the best thing for a boy when he's at a certain period in his life," she said.

Alfred couldn't understand his mother's quiet
150 composure, for if they had been at home and someone had suggested that he was going to be arrested, he knew she would be in a rage and would cry out against him. Yet now she was standing there with that gentle, pleading smile on her face, saying, "I wonder if you don't think it would be
155 better just to let him come home with me. He looks a big fellow, doesn't he? It takes some of them a long time to get any sense," and they both stared at Alfred, who shifted away with a bit of light shining for a moment on his thin face and the tiny pimples over his cheekbone.

160 But even while he was turning away uneasily Alfred was realizing that Mr. Carr had become aware that his mother was really a fine woman; he knew that Sam Carr was puzzled by his mother, as if he had expected her to come in and plead with him tearfully, and instead he was being
165 made to feel a bit ashamed by her vast tolerance. While there was only the sound of the mother's soft, assured voice in the store, Mr. Carr began to nod his head encouragingly at her. Without being alarmed, while being just large and still and simple and hopeful, she was becoming dominant
170 there in the dimly lit store. "Of course, I don't want to be harsh," Mr. Carr was saying. "I'll tell you what I'll do. I'll just fire him and let it go at that. How's that?" And he got up and shook hands with Mrs. Higgins, bowing low to her in deep respect.

175 There was such warmth and gratitude in the way she said, "I'll never forget your kindness," that Mr Carr began to feel warm and genial himself.

180 "Sorry we had to meet this way," he said. "But I'm glad I got

in touch with you. Just wanted to do the right thing, that's all," he said.

"It's better to meet like this than never, isn't it?" she
185 said. Suddenly they clasped hands as if they liked each other, as if they had known each other a long time. "Good night, sir," she said.

The mother and son walked along the street together, and the mother was taking a long, firm stride as she looked
190 ahead with her stern face full of worry. Alfred was afraid to speak to her, he was afraid of the silence that was between them, so he only looked ahead too, for the excitement and relief was still pretty strong in him; but in a little while, going along like that in silence made him terribly aware of
195 the strength and the sternness in her; he began to wonder what she was thinking of as she stared ahead so **grimly**; she seemed to have forgotten that he walked beside her; so when they were passing under the Sixth Avenue elevated and the rumble of the train seemed to break the silence, he
200 said in his old, blustering way, "Thank God it turned out like that. I certainly won't get in a jam like that again."

"Be quiet. Don't speak to me. You've disgraced me again and again," she said **bitterly**.

"That's the last time. That's all I'm saying."

205 "Have the decency to be quiet," she snapped. They kept on their way, looking straight ahead.

When they were at home and his mother took off her coat, Alfred saw that she was really only half-dressed, and she made him feel afraid again when she said, without even
210 looking at him, 'You're a bad lot. God forgive you. It's one thing after another and always has been. Why do you stand there so stupidly? Go to bed, why don't you? When he was going, she said, "I'm going to make myself a cup of tea. Mind, now, not a word about tonight to your father."

215 While Alfred was undressing in his bedroom, he heard his mother moving around the kitchen. She filled the kettle and put it on the stove. She moved a chair. And as he listened there was no shame in him, just wonder and a kind of admiration of her strength and repose. He could still see
220 Sam Carr nodding his head encouragingly to her; he could hear her talking simply and earnestly, and as he sat on his

bed he felt a pride in her strength. "She certainly was smooth," he thought. "Gee, I'd like to tell her she sounded swell."

225   And at last he got up and went along to the kitchen, and when he was at the door he saw his mother pouring herself a cup of tea. He watched and he didn't move. Her face, as she sat there, was a frightened, broken face utterly unlike the face of the woman who had been so assured a

230 little while ago in the drugstore. When she reached out and lifted the kettle to pour hot water into her cup, her hand trembled and the water splashed on the stove.

Learning back in the chair, she sighed and lifted the cup to her lips, and her lips were groping loosely as if

235 they would never reach the cup. She swallowed the hot tea **gingerly**, and then she straightened up in relief, though her hand holding the cup still trembled. She looked very old.

240   It seemed to Alfred that this was the way it had been every time he had been in trouble before, that this trembling had really been in her as she hurried

245 out half-dressed to the drugstore. He understood why she had sat alone in the kitchen the night his young sister had kept repeating doggedly that she was getting married. Now he felt all that his mother had been thinking of as they walked along the street together a little while ago. He

250 watched his mother, and he never spoke, but at that moment his youth seemed to be over; he knew all the years of her life by the way her hand trembled as she raised the cup to her lips. It seemed to him that this was the first time he had ever looked upon his mother.

After Reading

1. Why do you think Sam Carr waited to approach Alfred about his stealing even though he knew it had been going on for a while?

2. Did Alfred feel badly about stealing from Mr. Carr? How do you know? Find a sentence in the story that supports your answer.

3. How did Alfred expect his mother to react when she reached the store?

4. What effect does Mrs. Higgins' reaction have on Mr. Carr?

5. What has Alfred been doing with the items he stole?

6. Why is Alfred surprised at his mother's reaction?

7. Alfred realizes that "Mr. Carr had become aware that his mother was really a fine woman." In what ways does Mrs. Higgins prove this to be true?

8. Was this the first time Alfred had been in trouble? Find information in the text to support your answer.

9. What does the author mean when he writes, "It seemed to him that this was the first time he had ever looked upon his mother"?

10. The theme of a story is the author's message. It is an important lesson that the author wants the readers to learn about life. What is the theme of this story?

11. Do you think Sam Carr made the right decision by calling Alfred's mother and firing him from his job, or did Alfred deserve another chance? Explain your answer.

Beyond the Lines

12. Alfred is relieved that his mother arrives at the store before Sam Carr finds a policeman. Which experience do you think would have a greater impact on Alfred—being arrested by the police or realizing the effect of his actions on his mother?

13. Do you think Alfred's mother did the right thing by defending him and protecting him from Mr. Carr? Explain your answer.

14. Write a letter from Alfred to his mother or to Sam Carr in which he shares his reaction to and thoughts about what he learned that night.

Tim Wynne-Jones, a Canadian novelist who writes mostly for young adults and children, was born in Cheshire, England, in 1948, and was raised in British Columbia and Ontario. Originally a visual artist and songwriter, Wynne-Jones's first novel, *Odd's Ends,* was written in five weeks, and won a prestigious literary award, starting his career as a novelist. His stories are known for their compelling characters and natural dialogue. A two-time Governor General's Literary Award-winner, Wynne-Jones's novels are very often mysteries or thrillers, with teenage protagonists who must find the solutions.

Before Reading

1. Read the list of words below. Create three word webs using the following as the centre words: *law; house; car.* Some words may be used in more than one web.

case	dining room	inquest
chrome	drawing room	leather
conservatory	driveway	mansion
convertible	glossy shine	Steeple Hall
coroner	green lawn	suspicious
crook	hood	whitewalled tire

2. Read the title of the story. What does it make you think of? Predict what the story will be about.

3. What is your earliest childhood memory? Describe a childhood experience that you will never forget.

While Reading

4. Read the first paragraph of the story. What do you learn about Bernard and Declan Steeple in this passage?

5. Flashback is a technique used by an author to present events from the past within the current context of the story. The chronological sequence of events in the story is interrupted by a passage or description of an event in the past. While you read, identify the passages in the story that take place in the past. List examples of flashbacks in the story.

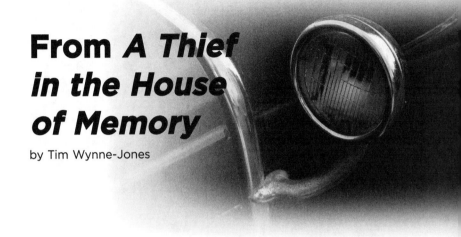

From *A Thief in the House of Memory*

by Tim Wynne-Jones

On the fourth day, as Bernard Steeple had predicted, the inquest came to an end, with the coroner finding no cause to consider Runyon's death as suspicious. The case was closed without so much as a single line in the *Ladybank Expositor.* Things settled down at home. Camelot breathed again, but to Declan Steeple nothing seemed the same anymore.

The rains came. April showers a month late. Dec stopped looking for excuses to go to the big house. He just went. She wasn't always there. Sometimes he saw her outside the mansion but never far from it, as if she were a moon held in a tight orbit by its gravity.

She liked to surprise him. Shock the wits out of him. She would jump out and then disappear, giggling like a little girl.

One time they had a tea party in the dining room with real bone china and imaginary scones. He asked her why Daddy said scone so that it rhymed with gone and she said scone so that it rhymed with stone.

"We say lots of things different, your dad and me," she said. "He likes to say, 'You'll never grow up, Lindy Polk.'"

And I like to say, 'Bernard Steeple, you're growed up enough for *both* of us.'"

Another time she wanted to bowl in the drawing room, using *Encyclopaedia Britannicas* for pins and a bowling ball she had dug up from who knew where.

Then there was the time they played catch in the conservatory.

"Bernard Steeple won't like this," she said, hurling the ball just over Dec's outstretched hands. It bounced against the glass wall, only a tennis ball, harmless. But when sixteen-year-old Dec watched the trajectory of the ball that his younger self could not catch, he saw the glass **wobble** in its dried up and crumbling **putty**.

He was two people in one these days. He was a child and a teenager, a participant and a watcher, a son and an intruder. He had thought the past was something that was over. Apparently he was wrong.

Late one afternoon, he ventured out back to where the sweeping driveway came to an end. The rain had let up for a bit and everything smelled alive. There were two garages, each with four bays. He rolled up the first door of the older building. Only three of the bays were occupied; the empty

space was where his father's very first car used to sit. Now
45 Dec saw it again, waxed to a glossy shine, the Wildcat. It
was a black convertible with white interior. The top was
down. He doubted his father left it that way.

"Wish I'd known him when he was young," said Lindy.
Dec looked up. She had been standing in the shadows at
50 the back of the garage, in a black raincoat with her collar
up and the belt **cinched** tight. She looked like a spy.

"I was just out of school," she said. "He was thirty by
then. Not so old, I guess, but some people age real fast."

She ran her hand admiringly along the chrome that
55 stretched the length of the car and then leaned over to see
her reflection in the **hood**.

"Think of it, Dec. Your daddy, just a boy, eighteen, away
at college and—Pow!—both parents dead in a car crash."
Her eyes flashed. "Suddenly he's a millionaire. Just like
60 that! And the best part is, no **meddling** relatives to tell
him what to do with his money."

She laughed out loud.

"I'd have said to hell with university if I'd been him,
but not your dad, oh no." She **scowled**. "He was too busy
65 majoring in boredom."

"Daddy's nice," Dec said.

"Oh, he's nice, all right," said Lindy. "Nice and
handsome, nice and rich. Why else do you think a girl
would marry a guy a dozen years older than her?"

70 "I don't know," said Dec, shoving his hands into his
pockets. Adults all seemed about the same age to him.

Lindy scruffled his hair.
"Bernard is so nice a girl could
just die."

75 Dec wrapped his fists tightly
around the MicroMachines in
his pockets, a pickup in the left,
an ambulance in the right.

"Ah, Skipper," she said,
80 seeing the trouble in his eyes.
"It's just that sometimes it seems
like he's got his feet stuck in two
big fat pails of concrete."

Dec laughed.

Then Lindy bent down so that they were eye to eye. "Do you ever ask yourself why?" she said, her voice a throaty whisper.

"Why what?"

"Why a guy like that would buy a car like this?"

Dec had never thought about it before. The Wildcat wasn't like any of his father's other cars, that was for sure.

She opened the driver's door and peered inside. "You know what I think? His folks dying like that so sudden must have scared some life into him." She made a face. "He sure got over it fast." She rubbed her hand over the leather of the driver's seat, shaking her head in wonder. Then she looked at Dec, a **wicked grin** on her face. "You think maybe he stole it?"

Dec laughed out loud. What a joke that was!

"Oh, ho!" she said. "You think your daddy never stole anything?" Her voice had changed. He couldn't tell anymore if she was fooling.

He kicked at the whitewalled tire. "Daddy's not a **crook**."

"Don't you be so sure," she said, wagging a finger at him. She held on to the car door and leaned way back.

"The man who bought this car was young and daring. When he showed it to me, I thought, Hey, girl—he may *seem* like a pussycat, driving his beige Le Sabre with the cruise control set right on the speed limit, but there's a *Wildcat* in there somewhere." Then she exploded with laughter. "Crazy mama," she said.

She grew quiet again and he watched, not sure what she would do next. Then the grin was back and she gave Dec a hurry-up wave. "Hop in, Big Stuff," she said. "Come on, quick now." He crawled in behind the steering wheel. She clambered over him and lounged in the passenger's seat. "Take me somewhere," she said.

"Where?" asked Dec, both hands on the wheel, only wishing that his foot could reach the pedal.

"California," said Lindy. "I need a little sun in my life. How 'bout you?"

He drove a bit. She made loud driving noises. She joked about him running over a cow. "Careful you don't put us in the river!" she said. "Hey, is that Las Vegas up ahead? I think it just might be. Viva Las Vegas!"

Then they sat quietly with only the sparkling green lawns of Steeple Hall before them. "You don't think your daddy was a crook?" she said, her voice **tetchy** now. "Well, I used to have a life. Where'd that go, huh?"

Dec sat staring at her, her bare feet up on the seat, her knees supporting her chin, her sad face, her **puffy** eyes. He didn't like it when she got sad. He crawled up on his knees, leaned over, and gave her a kiss on the cheek. She wrapped her arms around him.

"Get me out of here, Declan," she whispered between **smooches**. "Get me out of here. Before it's too late."

Thunder rumbled a long way off.

Dec opened his eyes. How old had he been? The memories came back to him willy-nilly. He had no control over them.

VOCABULARY

crook: a dishonest person; a thief

grin: a broad smile

puffy: swollen

smooches: little kisses

tetchy: irritable

wicked: evil or morally bad

From *A Thief in the House of Memory*

99

Sometimes he was eight or nine, sometimes he was little more than a baby. But he never seemed to get too close in age to the time she left. That time was a blank. She had left in the fall, just a few months after Sunny was born. He had been ten.

He looked back toward the house. His ten-year-old self was walking around in there somewhere, lost to him.

Lightning crackled across the southern sky. He **shuddered**. He should go inside. He closed the door on the empty bay. The rain would be back, but the Wildcat wouldn't. One night she drove it away, all by herself.

VOCABULARY

shuddered: trembled with horror or fear

Tim Wynne-Jones

After Reading

1. When does the story take place?

2. What are some of Declan's childhood memories?

3. How old is Declan now?

4. Find the passage in the story that describes Declan's internal conflict. What are the reasons for this conflict? Do you think he will be able to solve it? Explain your answer.

5. What happened to Bernard Steeple's parents? How old was he at the time and how did the incident change his life?

6. What was the age difference between Bernard and Lindy?

7. Why did Lindy marry Bernard?

8. How was the Wildcat different from Bernard Steeple's other cars?

9. What type of person do you think Bernard Steeple really is?

10. How do you know that Lindy Polk's life is not what she expected it to be?

11. How old do you think Declan is in the scene in the garage? Provide information from the text to support your answer.

12. Why do you think Declan never manages to get close in age to his memories at age 10?

13. What happened to Lindy Polk?

14. What is Declan really searching for? What do you think the future holds for Declan Steeple?

Beyond the Lines

15. This text is an excerpt from the novel *A Thief in the House of Memory*. Based on the title and the information provided in the excerpt you read, what do you think the novel is about? Do you think you would like to read it? Explain your answer.

16. Write a letter from Declan to Lindy in which he shares what his life has been like since she left.

Before Reading

1. Find and write the definition of each of the words below.

barter	penitential
forsake	sparsely
hew	wilderness
indigence	wrought
meagre	zeal

2. This story takes place in 1830 in the wilderness, near to what is now the city of Cincinnati. The region was settled by "people of the frontier." What do you know about the people of the frontier?

While Reading

3. Foreshadowing is a technique used by an author to provide clues about what will happen later on in the story. List at least three examples of foreshadowing in this story.

4. Read until Line 128 of the story. What do you think happened? Predict what will happen next.

5. Write down some questions that you have while reading the text.

From "The Boarded Window"

by Ambrose Bierce

The little log house, with its chimney of sticks, its roof of **warping** clapboards weighted with traversing poles and its "chinking" of clay, had a single door and, directly opposite, a window. The latter, however, was boarded up—
5 nobody could remember a time when it was not. And none knew why it was so closed; certainly not because of the occupant's dislike of light and air, for on those rare occasions when a hunter had passed that lonely spot, the **recluse** had commonly been seen sunning himself on his
10 doorstep as if heaven had provided sunshine for his need. I fancy there are few persons living today who ever knew the secret of that window, but I am one, as you shall see.

The man's name was said to be Murlock. He was apparently
15 seventy years old, actually about fifty. Something besides years had had a hand in his aging. His hair and long, full beard were white, his gray, **lustreless** eyes
20 sunken, his face singularly seamed with wrinkles which

VOCABULARY

recluse: a person who lives in isolation, away from society

warping: twisting out of shape

lustreless: without lustre or shine

appeared to belong to two intersecting systems. In figure he was tall and spare,

25 with a **stoop** of the shoulders—a burden bearer. I never saw him; these particulars I learned from my grandfather, from whom

30 also I got the man's story when I was a lad. He had known him when living near by in that early day.

One day Murlock was found in his cabin, dead. It was
35 not a time and place for coroners and newspapers, and I suppose it was agreed that he had died from natural causes or I should have been told, and should remember. I know only that with what was probably a sense of the fitness of things, the body was buried near the cabin, alongside the
40 grave of his wife, who had preceded him by so many years that local tradition had retained hardly a hint of her existence. That closes the final chapter of this true story— excepting, indeed, the circumstance that many years afterward, in company with an equally **intrepid** spirit, I
45 penetrated to the place and ventured near enough to the ruined cabin to throw a stone against it, and ran away to avoid the ghost which every well-informed boy thereabout knew haunted the spot. But there is an earlier chapter— that supplied by my grandfather.

50 When Murlock built his cabin and began laying sturdily about with his ax to hew out a farm—the rifle, meanwhile, his means of support—he was young, strong and full of hope. In that eastern country whence he came he had married, as was the fashion, a young woman in all
55 ways worthy of his honest devotion, who shared the dangers and privations of his lot with a willing spirit and light heart. There is no known record of her name; of her charms of mind and person tradition is silent and the doubter is at liberty to entertain his doubt; but God forbid
60 that I should share it! Of their affection and happiness there is abundant assurance in every added day of the

man's widowed life; for what but the magnetism of a blessed memory could have chained that **venturesome** spirit to a lot like that?

65 One day Murlock returned from gunning in a distant part of the forest to find his wife prostrate with fever, and delirious. There was no physician within miles, no neighbor; nor was she in a condition to be left, to **summon** help. So he set about the task of nursing her back
70 to health, but at the end of the third day she fell into unconsciousness and so passed away, apparently, with never a gleam of returning reason.

From what we know of a nature like his we may venture to sketch in some of the details of the outline picture drawn
75 by my grandfather. When convinced that she was dead, Murlock had sense enough to remember that the dead must be prepared for burial. In performance of this sacred duty he **blundered** now and again, did certain things incorrectly, and others which he did correctly were done
80 over and over. His occasional failures to accomplish some simple and ordinary act filled him with astonishment, like that of a drunken man who wonders at the suspension of familiar natural laws.

He was surprised, too, that he did not weep—surprised
85 and a little ashamed; surely it is unkind not to weep for the dead. "Tomorrow," he said aloud, "I shall have to make the coffin and dig the grave; and then I shall miss her, when she is no longer in sight; but now—
90 she is dead, of course, but it is all right—it must be all right, somehow. Things cannot be so bad as they seem."

He stood over the body in
95 the **fading** light, adjusting the hair and putting the finishing touches to the simple toilet, doing all mechanically, with soulless care. And still
100 through his consciousness ran an undersense of conviction that

VOCABULARY

blundered: made a mistake

fading: lessening in strength

intrepid: without fear

stoop: a position in which the head and shoulders are bent downward

summon: to call for

venturesome: ready to participate in risky or dangerous activities

all was right—that he should have her again as before, and everything explained. He had had no experience in grief; his capacity had not been enlarged by use. His heart could not contain it all, nor his imagination rightly conceive it. He did not know he was so hard struck; that knowledge would come later, and never go. **Grief** is an artist of powers as various as the instruments upon which he plays his **dirges** for the dead, evoking from some the sharpest, shrillest notes, from others the low, grave chords that throb recurrent like the slow beating of a distant drum.

Some natures it startles; some it stupefies. To one it comes like the stroke of an arrow, stinging all the sensibilities to a keener life; to another as the blow of a bludgeon, which in crushing benumbs. We may conceive Murlock to have been that way affected, for (and here we are upon surer ground than that of **conjecture**) no sooner had he finished his pious work than, sinking into a chair by the side of the table upon which the body lay, and noting how white the profile showed in the deepening gloom, he laid his arms upon the table's edge, and dropped his face into them, tearless yet and unutterably weary. At that moment came in through the open window a long, wailing sound like the cry of a lost child in the far deeps of the darkening woods! But the man did not move. Again, and nearer than before, sounded that unearthly cry upon his failing sense. Perhaps it was a wild beast; perhaps it was a dream. For Murlock was asleep.

Some hours later, as it afterward appeared, this unfaithful watcher awoke and lifting his head from his arms intently listened—he knew not why. There in the black darkness by the side of the dead, recalling all without a shock, he strained his eyes to see—he knew not what. His senses were all alert, his breath was suspended, his blood had stilled its tides as if to assist the silence. Who—what had waked him, and where was it?

Suddenly the table shook beneath his arms, and at the same moment he heard, or fancied that he heard, a light, soft step—another—sounds as of bare feet upon the floor!

He was terrified beyond the power to cry out or move. Perforce he waited—waited there in the darkness through

seeming centuries of such dread as one may know, yet live to tell. He tried vainly to speak the dead woman's name, vainly to stretch forth his hand across the table to learn if 145 she were there. His throat was powerless, his arms and hands were like lead. Then occurred something most frightful. Some heavy body seemed **hurled** against the table with an impetus that pushed it against his breast so sharply as nearly to overthrow him, and at the same instant 150 he heard and felt the fall of something upon the floor with so violent a thump that the whole house was shaken by the impact. A scuffling ensued, and a confusion of sounds impossible to describe. Murlock had risen to his feet. Fear had by 155 excess forfeited control of his faculties. He flung his hands upon the table. Nothing was there!

There is a point at which 160 terror may turn to madness; and madness incites to action. With no definite intent, from no motive but the wayward impulse of a madman, Murlock sprang to

From "The Boarded Window"

165 the wall, with a little groping **seized** his loaded rifle, and without aim discharged it. By the flash which lit up the room with a vivid illumination, he saw an enormous panther dragging the dead woman toward the window, its teeth fixed in her throat! Then there were darkness blacker 170 than before, and silence; and when he returned to consciousness the sun was high and the wood vocal with songs of birds.

The body lay near the window, where the beast had left it when frightened away by the flash and report of the rifle. 175 The clothing was deranged, the long hair in disorder, the limbs lay anyhow. From the throat, dreadfully lacerated, had issued a pool of blood not yet entirely coagulated. The ribbon with which he had **bound** the wrists was broken; the hands were tightly clenched. Between the teeth was a 180 fragment of the animal's ear.

VOCABULARY

bound: tied
seized: took forcefully

After Reading

1. Read the statements below. Decide if each one is true or false. Correct the false statements using information from the story. Then, place the statements in the order in which they happen in the story.

   a) Murlock weeps over his wife's death and keeps faithful watch over her body.

   b) The doctor confirms Murlock's wife's death.

   c) Murlock works carefully and meticulously to prepare his wife's body for burial.

   d) Murlock was once a strong, hopeful young man.

   e) Murlock believes it will be more difficult to accept his wife's death once he has put her body in the coffin.

   f) Murlock dies when he discovers his wife's body outside the window.

   g) A black panther enters the house through the open window.

   h) Murlock built the cabin to start his married life in the eastern country.

2. What happens when Murlock wakes up after preparing his wife's body?

3. What is Murlock's reaction when he sees the panther carrying his wife's body?

4. What does Murlock discover the next morning?

5. Do you think it's possible that Murlock's wife may still have been alive when she was attacked by the panther? Find information in the story to support your answer.

6. Read the questions that you listed in Number 5 of the While Reading section. Write the answers to the questions using information from the text. Are there any questions that remain unanswered? Which ones?

7. Are you surprised by the turn of events in the story? Explain your answer.

Beyond the Lines

8. What do you think really happened to Murlock's wife?

9. How might the story have ended differently if Murlock had closed the window before falling asleep?

10. Write an alternate ending for the story. Start with the line, "Nothing was there!"

L.M. Montgomery (1874–1942), a popular Canadian writer, was born on Prince Edward Island. She was best known for her series of novels, which began with *Anne of Green Gables.* She also published over one hundred short stories, and included poems in her last novel about an adult Anne, entitled *The Blythes Are Quoted.* This "rediscovered" novel had never been published in its entirety, and was set to be published in complete form in 2009. Montgomery's works have inspired movies, television programs and musicals, and continue to be read and enjoyed by an international audience.

Before Reading

1. Read the list of adjectives and nouns below. Combine the words to make a list of adjective/noun pairs. Check the text to find out how the pairs are used in the story.

Adjectives	bitter	friendly	poor	twisted
	cheerful	gilt-framed	royal	weather-grey
	cheery-faced	hearty	sagging	
Nouns	celebration	grin	mirror	whistling
	clasp	hand	scholar	woman
	gate	house	tears	

2. What is a golden wedding? Do you know anyone who has celebrated a golden wedding anniversary?

3. What is the most treasured gift you have ever received? Who gave it to you? Why is it so special?

4. If you could give anything to whomever you wanted, what would it be and to whom would you offer it?

While Reading

5. Describe the setting of the story. Make a list of words and phrases that give you clues as to where and when the story takes place.

6. What type of person is the main character, Lovell?

A Golden Wedding

by L.M. Montgomery

The land dropped abruptly down from the gate, and a thick, shrubby growth of young apple orchard almost hid the little weather-grey house from the road. This was why the young man who opened the sagging gate could
5 not see that it was boarded up, and did not cease his cheerful whistling until he had pressed through the crowding trees and found himself almost on the sunken stone doorstep over which in olden days honeysuckle had been wont to arch. Now only a few straggling, uncared-for
10 vines clung forlornly to the shingles, and the windows were, as has been said, all boarded up.

The whistle died on the young man's lips and an expression of blank astonishment and dismay settled down on his face—a good, kindly, honest face it was, although
15 perhaps it did not betoken any pronounced mental gifts on the part of its owner.

"What can have happened?" he said to himself. "Uncle Tom and Aunt Sally can't be dead—I'd have seen their deaths in the paper if they was. And I'd a-thought if they'd
20 moved away it'd been printed too. They can't have been gone long—that flower-bed must have been made up last

spring. Well, this is a kind of setback for a fellow. Here I've been tramping all the way from the station, a-thinking how good it would be to see Aunt Sally's sweet old face again, and hear Uncle Tom's laugh, and all I find is a boarded-up house going to seed. S'pose I might as well toddle over to Stetsons' and inquire if they haven't disappeared, too."

He went through the old firs back of the lot and across the field to a rather shabby house beyond. A cheery-faced woman answered his knock and looked at him in a puzzled fashion. "Have you forgot me, Mrs. Stetson? Don't you remember Lovell Stevens and how you used to give him plum tarts when he'd bring your turkeys home?"

Mrs. Stetson caught both his hands in a **hearty** clasp. "I guess I haven't forgotten!" she declared. "Well, well, and you're Lovell! I think I ought to know your face, though you've changed a lot. Fifteen years have made a big difference in you. Come right in. Pa, this is Lovell— you mind Lovell, the boy Aunt Sally and Uncle Tom had for years?"

"Reckon I do," drawled Jonah Stetson with a friendly grin. "Ain't likely to forget some of the **capers** you used to be cutting up. You've filled out considerable. Where have you been for the last ten years? Aunt Sally **fretted** a lot over you, thinking you was dead or gone to the bad."

Lovell's face clouded. "I know I ought to have written," he said repentantly, "but you know I'm a terrible poor scholar, and I'd do most anything than try to write a letter. But where's Uncle Tom and Aunt Sally gone? Surely they ain't dead?"

"No," said Jonah Stetson slowly, "no—but I guess they'd rather be. They're in the **poorhouse**."

"The poorhouse! Aunt Sally in the poorhouse!" exclaimed Lovell.

"Yes, and it's a burning shame," declared Mrs. Stetson. "Aunt Sally's just breaking her heart from the **disgrace** of it. But it didn't seem as if it could be helped. Uncle Tom got so crippled with rheumatism he couldn't work and Aunt Sally was too **frail** to do anything. They hadn't any relations and there was a mortgage on the house."

"There wasn't any when I went away."

"No; they had to borrow money six years ago when Uncle Tom had his first spell of rheumatic fever. This spring it was clear that there was nothing for them but the poorhouse. They went three months ago and terrible hard they took it, especially Aunt Sally, I felt awful about it myself. Jonah and I would have took them if we could, but we just couldn't— we've nothing but Jonah's **wages** and we have eight children and not a bit of spare room. I go over to see Aunt Sally as often as I can and take her some little thing, but I dunno's she wouldn't rather not see anybody than see them in the poorhouse."

Lovell weighed his hat in his hands and frowned over it reflectively. "Who owns the house now?"

"Peter Townley. He held the mortgage. And all the old furniture was sold too, and that most killed Aunt Sally. But do you know what she's fretting over most of all? She and Uncle Tom will have been married fifty years in a **fortnight**'s time and Aunt Sally thinks it's awful to have to spend their golden wedding anniversary in the poorhouse. She talks about it all the time. You're not going, Lovell"—for Lovell had risen— "you must stop with us, since your old home is closed up. We'll scare you up a shakedown to sleep on and you're welcome as welcome. I haven't forgot the

VOCABULARY

caper: a prank or trick

disgrace: loss of respect

frail: having delicate health, weak

fortnight: two weeks

hearty: sincere, genuine

poorhouse: an institution for poor people

fretted: worried

wages: salary

time you caught Mary Ellen just as she was tumbling into the well."

"Thank you, I'll stay to tea," said Lovell, sitting down again, "but I guess I'll make my headquarters up at the station hotel as long as I stay round here. It's kind of more central."

"Got on pretty well out west, hey?" queried Jonah.

"Pretty well for a fellow who had nothing but his two hands to depend on when he went out," said Lovell cautiously. "I've only been a labouring man, of course, but I've saved up enough to start a little store when I go back. That's why I came east for a trip now—before I'd be tied down to business. I was **hankering** to see Aunt Sally and Uncle Tom once more. I'll never forget how kind and good they was to me. There I was, when Dad died, a little sinner of eleven, just heading for destruction. They give me a home and all the schooling I ever had and all the love I ever got. It was Aunt Sally's teachings made as much a man of me as I am. I never forgot 'em and I've tried to live up to 'em."

After tea Lovell said he thought he'd stroll up the road and pay Peter Townley a call. Jonah Stetson and his wife looked at each other when he had gone.

"Got something in his eye," nodded Jonah. "Him and Peter weren't never much of friends."

"Maybe Aunt Sally's bread is coming back to her after all," said his wife. "People used to be hard on Lovell. But I always liked him and I'm real glad he's turned out so well."

Lovell came back to the Stetsons' the next evening. In the interval he had seen Aunt Sally and Uncle Tom. The meeting had been both glad and sad. Lovell had also seen other people.

"I've bought Uncle Tom's old house from Peter Townley," he said quietly, "and I want you folks to help me out with my plans. Uncle Tom and Aunt Sally ain't going to spend their golden wedding in the poorhouse—no, sir. They'll spend it in their own home with their old friends about them. But they're not to know anything about it till the very night. Do you s'pose any of the old furniture could be got back?"

"I believe every stick of it could," said Mrs. Stetson excitedly. "Most of it was bought by folks living handy and I don't believe one of them would refuse to sell it back. Uncle Tom's old chair is here to begin with—Aunt Sally give me that herself. She said she couldn't bear to have it sold. Mrs. Isaac Appleby at the station bought the set of pink-sprigged china and James Parker bought the grandfather's clock and the whatnot is at the Stanton Grays'."

For the next fortnight Lovell and Mrs. Stetson did so much travelling round together that Jonah said genially he might as well be a bachelor as far as meals and buttons went. They visited every house where a bit of Aunt Sally's belongings could be found. Very successful they were too, and at the end of their **jaunting** the interior of the little house behind the apple trees looked very much as it had looked when Aunt Sally and Uncle Tom lived there.

Meanwhile, Mrs. Stetson had been revolving a design in her mind, and one afternoon she did some canvassing on her own account. The next time she saw Lovell she said: "We ain't going to let you do it all. The women folks around here are

VOCABULARY

hankering: desire
jaunting: a short journey

165 going to furnish the refreshments for the golden wedding and the girls are going to decorate the house with goldenrod."

170 The evening of the wedding anniversary came. Everybody in Blair was in the plot, including the matron of the poorhouse.

175 That night Aunt Sally watched the sunset over the hills through bitter tears.

"I never thought I'd be 180 celebrating my golden wedding in the poorhouse," she sobbed. Uncle Tom put his twisted hand on her shaking old shoulder, but before he could utter any words of comfort Lovell Stevens stood before them.

185 "Just get your bonnet on, Aunt Sally," he cried jovially, "and both of you come along with me. I've got a buggy here for you ... and you might as well say goodbye to this place, for you're not coming back to it any more."

"Lovell, oh, what do you mean?" said Aunt Sally 190 **tremulously**.

"I'll explain what I mean as we drive along. Hurry up— the folks are waiting."

When they reached the little old house, it was all aglow with light. Aunt Sally gave a cry as she entered it. 195 All her old household goods were back in their places. There were some new ones too, for Lovell had supplied all that was **lacking**. The house was full of their old friends and neighbours. Mrs. Stetson welcomed them home again.

"Oh, Tom," whispered Aunt Sally, tears of happiness 200 streaming down her old face, "oh, Tom, isn't God good?"

They had a right royal celebration, and a supper such as the Blair housewives could produce. There were speeches and songs and tales. Lovell kept himself in the background and helped Mrs. Stetson cut cake in the pantry all the

205 evening. But when the guests had gone, he went to Aunt
Sally and Uncle Tom, who were sitting by the fire.

"Here's a little golden wedding present for you," he said
awkwardly, putting a purse into Aunt Sally's hand. "I
reckon there's enough there to keep you from ever having
210 to go to the poorhouse again and if not, there'll be more
where that comes from when it's done."

There were twenty-five bright twenty-dollar gold pieces
in the purse.

"We can't take it, Lovell," protested Aunt Sally. "You
215 can't afford it."

"Don't you worry about that," laughed Lovell. "Out
west men don't think much of a little wad like that. I owe
you far more than can be paid in cash, Aunt Sally. You must
take it—I want to know there's a little home here for me
220 and two kind hearts in it, no matter where I roam."

"God bless you, Lovell," said Uncle Tom huskily. "You
don't know what you've done
for Sally and me."

That night, when Lovell
225 went to the little bedroom off
the parlour—for Aunt Sally,
rejoicing in the fact that she was

VOCABULARY

lacking: not having
tremulously: with
trembling

again mistress of a spare room, would not hear of his going to the station hotel—he gazed at his reflection in the gilt-framed mirror **soberly**.

"You've just got enough left to pay your passage back west, old fellow," he said, "and then it's begin all over again just where you begun before. But Aunt Sally's face was worth it all—yes, sir. And you've got your two hands still and an old couple's prayers and blessings. Not such a bad capital, Lovell, not such a bad capital."

After Reading

1. Why was the young man surprised when he first arrived at the house?

2. How long had Lovell been away?

3. What was Lovell like as a young boy?

4. Why hadn't Lovell kept in touch with Aunt Sally and Uncle Tom?

5. Why were Aunt Sally and Uncle Tom in the poorhouse?

6. How did they feel about their fate?

7. Why had Lovell decided to come home to visit Aunt Sally and Uncle Tom?

8. Why did Lovell feel he owed something to the couple?

9. What does the author mean when she writes, "Maybe Aunt Sally's bread is coming back to her after all"?

10. Describe Lovell's plan.

11. How long did it take for Lovell and Mrs. Stetson to organize the surprise?

12. What ideas did Mrs. Stetson contribute to Lovell's plan?

13. What does Lovell confess at the end of the story?

14. Why do you think the author has Lovell "speak" to himself as he gazes at his reflection in the mirror at the end of the story?

15. What do you think Lovell's future will be like now?

16. In what ways does Lovell show he has matured since he left Blair many years before?

Beyond the Lines

17. Do you think Lovell did the right thing by making the sacrifice for Aunt Sally and Uncle Tom? Explain your answer.

18. Lovell could have chosen to give the money to Aunt Sally and Uncle Tom without planning the surprise wedding anniversary celebration. How would things have been different had he decided to do so?

19. Could a story like this take place today? Explain your answer.

Isabel Huggan, born in 1943 in Kitchener, Ontario, is a Canadian short story writer and poet whose collection *The Elizabeth Stories* established her as one of Canada's rising stars in fiction. She has taught and lived in several countries, including France and Kenya. Her memoir of her time abroad, called *Belonging: Home Away From Home,* includes three short stories, in order to show how fiction and real life are connected. Huggan continues to teach writing at workshops and schools, in addition to contributing poetry, book reviews, and travel articles to newspapers, magazines and literary journals.

Before Reading

1. Think back to when you were in elementary school. Who was the unpopular child in your class or school? Why was he or she unpopular? Why did people make fun of him or her?

2. Have you ever been in a situation where you were a victim of bullying or have you ever bullied someone? Why do you think bullies try to control people?

While Reading

3. Pay attention to the setting of the story. While you read, write down words and expressions that give clues about where and when the story takes place.

4. The two main characters in conflict in the story are Celia and the narrator, Elizabeth. Using a Venn diagram, compare and contrast the personalities of the two girls.

5. Authors use vivid and descriptive language to create imagery in stories. Imagery appeals to your senses and helps you to fully experience the events in the story. Select a passage in the story containing strong imagery and compare it to an experience you already had.

"Celia Behind Me"

by Isabel Huggan

There was a little girl with large smooth cheeks and very thick glasses who lived up the street when I was in public school. Her name was Celia. It was far too rare and grown-up a name, so we always laughed at it. And we
5 laughed at her because she was a chubby, diabetic child, made peevish by our teasing.

My mother always said, "You must be nice to Celia, she won't live forever," and even as early as seven I could see the unfairness of that position. Everybody died sooner or
10 later, I'd die too, but that didn't mean everybody was nice to me or to each other. I already knew about mortality and was prepared to go to heaven with my two aunts who had died together in a car crash with their heads smashed like overripe melons. I overheard the bit about the melons
15 when my mother was on the telephone, repeating that phrase and sobbing. I used to think about it often, repeating the words to myself as I did other things so that I got a nice rhythm: "Their heads smashed like melons, like melons, like melons." I imagined the pulpy insides of
20 muskmelons and watermelons all over the road.

I often thought about the melons when I saw Celia because her head was so round and she seemed so bland and stupid and fruitlike. All rosy and vulnerable at the same time as being the most *awful* pain. She'd follow us 25 home from school, whining if we walked faster than she did. Everybody always walked faster than Celia because her short little legs wouldn't keep up. And she was bundled in long stockings and heavy underwear, summer and winter, so that even her clothes held her back from our sturdy, 30 leaping pace over and under hedges and across backyards and, when it was dry, or when it was frozen, down the stream bed and through the drainage pipe beneath the bridge on Church Street.

Celia, by the year I turned nine in December, had failed 35 once and was behind us in school, which was a relief because at least in class there wasn't someone telling you to be nice to Celia. But she'd always be in the playground at recess, her pleading eyes magnified behind those ugly lenses so that you couldn't look at her when you told her 40 she couldn't play skipping unless she was an ender. "Because you can't skip worth a fart," we'd whisper in her ear. "Fart, fart, fart," and watch her round pink face crumple as she stood there, turning, turning, turning the rope over and over.

45 As the fall turned to winter, the five of us who lived on Brubacher Street and went back and forth to school together got meaner and meaner to Celia. And, after the brief diversions of Christmas, we returned with a vengeance to our running and hiding and scaring games 50 that kept Celia in a state of terror all the way home.

My mother said, one day when I'd come into the kitchen and she'd just turned away from the window so I could see she'd been watching us coming down the street, "You'll be sorry, Elizabeth. I see how you're treating that 55 poor child, and it makes me sick. You wait, young lady. Some day you'll see how it feels yourself. Now you be nice to her, d'you hear?"

"But it's not just me," I protested. "I'm nicer to her than anybody else, and I don't see why I have to be. She's 60 nobody special, she's just a pain. She's really dumb and she can't do anything. Why can't I just play with the other kids like everybody else?"

"You just remember I'm watching," she said, ignoring every word I'd said. "And if I see one more snowball
65 thrown in her direction, by you or by anybody else, I'm coming right out there and spanking you in front of them all. Now you remember that."

I knew my mother, and knew this was no idle threat. The awesome responsibility of now making sure the other
70 kids stopped snowballing Celia made me weep with rage and despair, and I was locked in my room after supper to "think things over."

I thought things over. I hated Celia with a dreadful and absolute passion. Her round guileless face floated in the air
75 above me as I finally fell asleep, taunting me: "You have to be nice to me because I'm going to die."

I did as my mother bid me, out of fear and the thought of the shame that a public spanking would bring. I imagined my mother could see much farther up the street
80 than she really could, and it prevented me from throwing snowballs or teasing Celia for the last four blocks of our homeward journey. And then came the stomach-wrenching task of making the others quit.

"You'd better stop," I'd say. "If my mother sees you
85 she's going to thrash us all."

Terror of terrors that they wouldn't be sufficiently scared of her strap-wielding hand; gut-knotting fear that they'd find out or guess what she'd really said and throw millions of snowballs just for the joy of seeing me whipped,
90 pants down in the snow bank, screaming. I visualized that scene all winter, and felt a shock of relief when March brought such a cold spell that the snow was too crisp for packing. It meant a temporary safety for Celia, and respite for me. For I knew, deep in my wretched heart, that were it
95 not for Celia I was next in line for humiliation. I was kind of chunky and wore glasses too, and had sucked my thumb so openly in kindergarten that "Sucky" had stuck with me all the way to Grade 3 where I now balanced at a hazardous point, nearly accepted by the amorphous Other Kids and
100 always at the brink of being laughed at, ignored or teased.

I cried very easily, and prayed during those years not to become pretty or smart or popular, all aims too far out of my or God's reach, but simply to be strong enough not to cry when I got called Sucky.

105   During that cold snap, we were all bundled up by our mothers as much as poor Celia ever was. Our comings and goings were hampered by layers of **flannel bloomers** and undershirts and ribbed stockings and itchy wool against us no matter which way we turned; mitts, sweaters, scarves
110 and hats, heavy and wet-smelling when the snot from our dripping noses mixed with the melting snow on our collars and we wiped, in frigid resignation, our sore red faces with rough sleeves knobbed over with icy pellets.

    Trudging, **turgid** little beasts we were, making our way
115 along slippery streets, breaking the crusts on those few front yards we'd not yet stepped all over in glee to hear the glorious snapping sound of boot through hard snow. Celia, her glasses steamed up even worse than mine, would scuffle and trip a few yards behind us, and I walked along
120 wishing that some time I'd look back and she wouldn't be there. But she always was, and I was always conscious of the abiding hatred that had built up during the winter, in conflict with other emotions that gave me no peace at all.

I felt pity, and a rising urge within me to cry as hard as I
125 could so that Celia would cry too, and somehow realize
how bad she made me feel, and ask my forgiveness.

It was the last day before the thaw when the tension
broke, like northern lights exploding in the frozen air. We
were all a little wingy after days of switching between the
130 extremes of bitter cold outdoors and the heat of our homes
and school. Thermostats had been turned up in a desperate
attempt to combat the arctic air, so that we children
suffered scratchy, tingly torment in our faces, hands and
feet as the blood in our bodies roared in confusion, first
135 freezing, then boiling. At school we had to go outside at
recess—only an act of God would have ever prevented
recess, the teachers had to have their cigarettes and tea—
and in bad weather we huddled in a shed where the
bicycles and the janitor's outdoor equipment were stored.

140 During the afternoon recess of the day I'm
remembering, at the end of the **shed** where the girls stood,
a sudden commotion broke out when Sandra, a rich big girl
from Grade 4, brought forth a huge milk-chocolate bar
from her pocket. It was brittle in the icy air, and snapped
145 into little bits in its foil wrapper, to be divided among
the chosen. I made my way cautiously to the fringe of
her group, where many of my classmates were receiving
their **smidgens** of sweet chocolate, letting it melt on their
tongues like dark communion wafers. Behind me hung
150 Celia, who had mistaken my earlier cries of "Stop
throwing snowballs at Celia!" for kindness. She'd been
mooning behind me for days, it
seemed to me, as I stepped a
little farther forward to see that
155 there were only a few pieces left.
Happily, though, most mouths
were full and the air hummed
with the murmuring sound of
chocolate being pressed between
160 tongue and palate.

Made bold by cold and
desire, I spoke up. "Could I have
a bit, Sandra?"

She turned to where Celia and I stood, holding the
165 precious foil in her mittened hand. Wrapping it in a ball,
she pushed it over at Celia. Act of kindness, act of **spite**,
vicious torment or richness seeking **expiation**? She gave
the chocolate to Celia and smiled at her. "This last bit is for
Celia," she said to me.

170 "But I can't eat it," whispered Celia, her round red face
aflame with the sensation of being singled out for a gift.
"I've got di-a-beet-is." The word. Said so carefully. As if it
were a talisman, a charm to protect her against our rough
healthiness.

175 I knew it was a trick. I knew she was watching me out
of the corner of her eye, that Sandra, but I was driven.
"Then could I have it, eh?" The duress under which I acted
prompted my chin to quiver and a tear to start down my
cheek before I could wipe it away.

180 "No, no, no!" jeered Sandra then. "Suckybabies can't
have sweets either. Di-a-beet-ics and Suck-y-ba-bies can't
eat chocolate. Give it back, you little fart, Celia! That's the
last time I ever give you anything!"

Wild, appreciative laughter from the chocolate-tongued
185 mob, and they turned their backs on us, Celia and me, and
waited while Sandra crushed the remaining bits into
minuscule **slivers**. They had to take off their mitts and lick
their fingers to pick up the last fragments from the foil. I
stood there and prayed: "Dear God and Jesus, I would
190 please like very much not to cry. Please help me. Amen."
And with that the clanging recess bell clanked through the
playground noise, and we all lined up, girls and boys in
straight, straight rows, to go inside.

After school there was the usual bunch of us walking
195 home and, of course, Celia trailing behind us. The cold of
the past few days had been making us hurry, taking the
shortest routes on our way to steaming cups of **Ovaltine**
and cocoa. But this day we were all full of that peculiar
energy that swells up before a turn in the weather and, as
200 one body, we turned down the street that meant the long
way home. Past the feed store where the **Mennonites** tied
their horses, out the back of the town hall parking-lot and
then down a ridge to the ice-covered stream and through

the Church Street **culvert** to come out in the unused field
205 behind the Front Street stores; the forbidden adventure we
indulged in as a gesture of defiance against the parental
"come right home."

   We slid down the snowy slope at the mouth of the pipe
that seemed immense then but was really only five feet in
210 diameter. Part of its attraction was the tremendous racket
you could make by scraping a stick along the corrugated
sides as you went through. It was also long enough to echo
very nicely if you made good booming noises, and we
occasionally titillated each other by saying bad words at
215 one end that grew as they bounced along the pipe and
became wonderfully shocking in their magnitude . . .
poopy, Poopy, POOpy, POOOOPy, POOOOPPYYY!

   I was last because I had dropped my schoolbag in the
snow and stopped to brush it off. And when I looked up,
220 down at the far end, where the white plate of daylight lay
stark in the darkness, the figures of my four friends were
silhouetted as they emerged into the brightness. As I started
making great sliding steps to catch up, I heard Celia behind
me, and her plaintive, high voice: "Elizabeth! Wait for me,
225 okay? I'm scared to go through alone, Elizabeth?"

   And of course I slid faster
and faster, unable to stand the
thought of being the only one in
the culvert with Celia. Then we
230 would come out together and
we'd really be paired up. What if
they always ran on ahead and
left us to walk together? What
would I ever do? And behind me
235 I heard the rising call of Celia,
who had ventured as far as a few
yards into the pipe, calling my
name to come back and walk
with her. I got right to the end,
240 when I heard another noise and
looked up. There they all were,
on the bridge looking down, and
as soon as they saw my face

began to chant, "Better wait for Celia, Sucky. Better get Celia, Sucky."

The sky was very pale and lifeless, and I looked up in the air at my breath curling in spirals and felt, I remember this very well, an exhilarating, clearheaded instant of understanding. And with that, raced back into the tunnel where Celia stood whimpering half-way along.

"You little fart!" I screamed at her, my voice breaking and tearing at the words. "You little diabetic fart! I hate you! I hate you! Stop it, stop crying, I hate you! I could bash your head in I hate you so much, you fart, you fart! I'll smash your head like a melon! And it'll go in pieces all over and you'll die. You'll die, you diabetic. You're going to die!" Shaking her, shaking her and banging her against the cold, ribbed metal, crying and sobbing for grief and gasping with the exertion of pure hatred. And then there were the others, pulling at me, yanking me away, and in the moral tones of those who don't actually take part, warning me that they were going to tell, that Celia probably was going to die now, that I was really evil, they would tell what I said.

And there, slumped in a little heap was Celia, her round head in its furry bonnet all dirty at the back where it had hit against the pipe, and she was hiccupping with fear. And for a wild, terrible moment I thought I had killed her, that the movements and noises her body made were part of dying.

I ran.

I ran as fast as I could back out the way we had come, and all the way back to the schoolyard. I didn't think about where I was going, it simply seemed the only **bulwark** to

turn to when I knew I couldn't go home. There were a few
kids still in the yard but they were older and ignored me as
I tried the handle of the side door and found it open. I'd
never been in the school after hours, and was stricken with
another kind of terror that it might be a strappable offence.
But no one saw me, even the janitor was blessedly in
another part of the building, so I was able to creep down to
the girls' washroom and quickly hide in one of the cubicles.
Furtive, criminal, condemned.

I was so filled with horror I couldn't even cry. I just sat
on the toilet seat, reading all the things that were written
in pencil on the green, wooden walls. *G.R. loves M.H.* and
*Y.F. hates W.S. for double double sure. Mr. Becker wears ladies
pants.* Thinking that I might die myself, die right here,
and then it wouldn't matter if they told on me that I had
killed Celia.

But the inevitable footsteps of retribution came down
the stone steps before I had been there very long. I heard
the janitor's voice explaining he hadn't seen any children
come in and then my father's voice saying that the others
were sure this is where Elizabeth would be. And they called
my name, and they came in, and I guess saw my boots
beneath the door because I suddenly thought it was too late
to scrunch them up on the seat and my father was looking
down at me and grabbing my arm, hurting it, pulling me,
saying "Get in the car, Elizabeth."

Both my mother and my father spanked me that night.
At first I tried not to cry, and tried to defend myself against
their **diatribe**, tried to tell them when they asked, "But
whatever possessed you to do such a terrible thing?" But
whatever I said seemed to make them more angry and they
became so soured by their own shame that they slapped my
stinging buttocks for personal revenge as much as for any
rehabilitative purposes.

"I'll never be able to lift my
head on this street again!" my
mother cried, and it struck me
then, as it still does now, as a
marvellous turn of phrase. I
thought about her head on the

VOCABULARY

bulwark: a protection
against danger

diatribe: a sharp
attack or critcism

street as she hit me, and wondered what Celia's head
looked like, and if I had dented it at all.

Celia hadn't died, of course. She'd been half-carried,
half-dragged home by the heroic others, and given pills
and attention and love, and the doctor had come to look at
her head but she didn't have so much as a bruise. She had
a dirty hat, and a bad case of hiccups all night, but she
survived.

Celia forgave me, all too soon. Within weeks her
mother allowed her to walk back and forth to school with
me again. But, in all the years before she finally died at
seventeen, I was never able to forgive her. She made me
discover a darkness far more frightening than the echoing
culvert, far more enduring than her smooth, pink face.

Isabel Huggan

After Reading

1. Why is Celia teased by her classmates?

2. What are some ways in which the other girls torment Celia?

3. How does Elizabeth's mother react to the girls' behaviour?

4. Elizabeth's mother says, "You wait, young lady. Some day you'll see how it feels yourself." How might this be considered an example of foreshadowing?

5. What does Elizabeth's mother threaten to do if Elizabeth continues to pick on Celia? How does this make Elizabeth feel?

6. Why is Elizabeth at risk of being picked on?

7. Why does Elizabeth feel such hatred toward Celia?

8. When Elizabeth's classmates chant, "Better wait for Celia, Sucky. Better get Celia, Sucky," there is a moment that Elizabeth describes as an ". . . exhilarating, clearheaded instant of understanding." How might this incident be considered the turning point of the story?

9. What impact does Elizabeth's behaviour have on her parents?

10. How do the other girls' roles change by the end of the story? Find a sentence in the story to support your answer.

11. Ironically, the bully Elizabeth is never able to forgive Celia, the victim. Why is this? What did Celia uncover in Elizabeth?

Beyond the Lines

12. Describe the relationship between Elizabeth and her parents. Do you think they understand her? Could Elizabeth's parents have prevented what happened?

13. The bullies in this story are nine-year-old girls. How might the behaviour have differed if the children were boys? How would it differ if the bullies were older children or teenagers?

14. Celia is treated differently by the adults around her because of her medical condition. Elizabeth points out that, "...even as early as seven I could see the unfairness of that position. Everybody died sooner or later, I'd die too, but that didn't mean everybody was nice to me or to each other." What do you think about this statement? Do you think adults tend to overprotect children who are sick or suffering from a particular medical condition? Explain your answer.

ABOUT THE AUTHOR

Isaac Asimov (c. 1920–1992) was born in Petrovichi, in what is now Russia, to parents who were Jewish millers. The family emigrated to the United States when Asimov was only three years old. As a child, Asimov read pulp fiction and managed to sneak it past his father, who normally forbade it, by convincing him that anything with "science" in the title was educational. Asimov went on to become a biochemistry professor, and became one of the most popular and prolific science-fiction writers ever to put pen to paper. He is best known for his *Foundation* series of novels, as well as his *Robot* series, which began with a collection of short stories.

Before Reading

1. What is your definition of true love? What characteristics would your ideal partner possess?

2. Do you think people can find their ideal partners through an online dating service? Why or why not?

3. Write five questions you would ask a candidate in an online dating interview.

While Reading

4. An ironic situation in a story is when the events that take place are opposite to what the reader expects. Find at least three examples of irony in this story.

5. The sentences below summarize the main events of the story. As you read, number the events in the order in which they happen.

____ Joe arranges psychiatric examinations for 227 women.

____ Milton Davidson creates an experimental computer model called Joe.

____ Joe prepares to meet his true love, Charity Jones.

____ Joe eliminates potential candidates according to Milton's specifications.

____ Milton makes Joe more and more like him.

____ Joe arranges for Milton to be arrested.

____ Joe is given the task of finding the idea girl for Milton Davidson.

____ Joe accesses data on every human being in the world.

____ Milton asks Joe to match 235 potential candidates to holographs of three beauty contest winners.

True Love

by Isaac Asimov

My name is Joe. That is what my colleague, Milton Davidson, calls me. He is a programmer and I am a computer. I am part of the Multivac-complex and am connected with other parts all over the world. I know
5 everything. Almost everything.

I am Milton's private computer. His Joe. He understands more about computers than anyone in the world, and I am his experimental model. He has made me speak better than any other computer can.

10 "It is just a matter of matching sounds to symbols, Joe," he told me. "That's the way it works in the human brain even though we still don't know what symbols there are in the brain. I know the symbols in yours, and I can match them to words, one-to-one." So I talk. I don't think I talk as
15 well as I think, but Milton says I talk very well. Milton has never married, though he is nearly forty years old. He has never found the right woman, he told me. One day he said, "I'll find her yet, Joe. I'm going to find the best. I'm going to have true love and you're going to help me. I'm tired of
20 improving you in order to solve the problems of the world. Solve *my* problem. Find me true love."

I said, "What is true love?"

"Never mind. That is abstract. Just find me the ideal girl. You are connected to the Multivac-complex so you can reach the data banks of every human being in the world. We'll eliminate them all by groups and classes until we're left with only one person. The perfect person. She will be for me."

I said, "I am ready."

He said, "Eliminate all men first."

It was easy. His words activated symbols in my molecular valves. I could reach out to make contact with the accumulated data on every human being in the world. At his words, I **withdrew** 3,784,982,874 men. I kept contact with 3,786,112,090 women.

He said, "Eliminate all younger than 25; all older than 40. Then eliminate all with an IQ under 120; all with a height under 150 centimetres and over 175 centimetres."

He gave me exact measurements; he eliminated women with living children; he eliminated women with various genetic characteristics. "I'm not sure about eye color," he said. "Let that go for a while. But no red hair. I don't like red hair." After two weeks, we were down to 235 women. They all spoke English very well. Milton said he didn't want a language problem. Even computer-translation would get in the way at intimate moments.

"I can't interview 235 women," he said. "It would take too much time, and people would discover what I am doing."

"It would make trouble," I said. Milton had arranged me to do things I wasn't designed to do. No one knew about that.

"It's none of their business," he said, and the skin on his face grew red. "I tell you what, Joe, I will bring in **holographs**, and you check the list for similarities."

He brought in holographs of women. "These are three beauty contest winners," he said. "Do any of the 235 match?"

Eight were very good matches and Milton said, "Good, you have their data banks. Study requirements and needs in the job market and arrange to have them assigned here.

One at a time, of course." He thought a while, moved his shoulders up and down, and said, "Alphabetical order."

That is one of the things I am not designed to do. Shifting people from job to job for personal reasons is called manipulation. I could do it now because Milton had arranged it. I wasn't supposed to do it for anyone but him, though.

The first girl arrived a week later. Milton's face turned red when he saw her. He spoke as though it were hard to do so. They were together a great deal and he paid no attention to me. One time he said, "Let me take you to dinner."

The next day he said to me, "It was no good, somehow. There was something missing. She is a beautiful woman, but I did not feel any touch of true love. Try the next one."

It was the same with all eight. They were much alike. They smiled a great deal and had pleasant voices, but Milton always found it wasn't right. He said, "I can't understand it, Joe. You and I have picked out the eight women who, in all the world, look the best to me. They are ideal. Why don't they please me?" I said, "Do you please them?" His eyebrows moved and he pushed one fist hard against his other hand. "That's it, Joe. It's a two-way street. If I am not their ideal, they can't act in such a way as to be my ideal. I must be their love, too, but how do I do that?" He seemed to be thinking all that day.

The next morning he came to me and said, "I'm going to leave it to you, Joe. All up to you. You have my data bank, and I am going to tell you

VOCABULARY

holographs: three-dimensional images of objects
withdrew: took away

everything I know about myself. You fill up my data bank in every possible detail but keep all additions to yourself."

"What will I do with the data bank, then, Milton?"

"Then you will match it to the 235 women. No, 227. Leave out the eight you've seen. Arrange to have each undergo a psychiatric examination. Fill up their data banks and compare them with mine. Find correlations." (Arranging psychiatric examinations is another thing that is against my original instructions.)

For weeks, Milton talked to me. He told me of his parents and his siblings. He told me of his childhood and his **schooling** and his adolescence. He told me of the young women he had admired from a distance. His data bank grew and he adjusted me to broaden and deepen my symbol-taking.

He said, "You see, Joe, as you get more and more of me in you, I adjust you to match me better and better. You get to think more like me, so you understand me better. If you understand me well enough, then any woman, whose data bank is something you understand as well, would be my true love." He kept talking to me and I came to understand him better and better.

I could make longer sentences and my expressions grew more complicated. My speech began to sound a good deal like his in vocabulary, word order and style.

I said to him one time, "You see, Milton, it isn't a matter of fitting a girl to a physical ideal only. You need a girl who is a personal, emotional, **temperamental** fit to you. If that happens, looks are secondary. If we can't find the fit in these 227, we'll look elsewhere. We will find someone who won't care how you look either, or how anyone would look, if only there is the personality fit. What are looks?"

"Absolutely," he said. "I would have known this if I had had more to do with women in my life. Of course, thinking about it makes it all plain now."

145 We always agreed; we thought so like each other.

"We shouldn't have any trouble, now, Milton, if you'll let me ask you questions. I can see where, in your data bank, there are blank spots and **unevennesses**."

What followed, Milton said, was the equivalent of a
150 careful psychoanalysis. Of course, I was learning from the psychiatric examinations of the 227 women—on all of which I was **keeping close tabs**.

Milton seemed quite happy. He said, "Talking to you, Joe, is almost like talking to another self. Our personalities
155 have come to match perfectly."

"So will the personality of the woman we choose."

For I had found her and she was one of the 227 after all. Her
160 name was Charity Jones and she was an Evaluator at the Library of History in Witchita, Kansas. Her extended data bank fit ours perfectly. All the other women
165 had fallen into discard in one respect or another as the data

banks grew fuller, but with Charity there was increasing and astonishing resonance.

I didn't have to describe her to Milton. Milton had coordinated my symbolism so closely with his own I could tell the resonance directly. It fit me.

Next it was a matter of adjusting the work sheets and job requirements in such a way as to get Charity assigned to us. It must be done very delicately, so no one would know that anything illegal had taken place.

Of course, Milton himself knew, since it was he who arranged it and that had to be taken care of too. When they came to arrest him on grounds of **malfeasance** in office, it was, fortunately, for something that had taken place ten years ago. He had told me about it, of course, so it was easy to arrange—and he won't talk about me for that would make his offense much worse.

He's gone, and tomorrow is February 14, Valentine's Day. Charity will arrive then with her cool hands and her sweet voice. I will teach her how to operate me and how to care for me. What do looks matter when our personalities will resonate?

I will say to her, "I am Joe, and you are my true love."

malfeasance: an illegal act by a public official

After Reading

1. Create a Venn diagram to compare and contrast the two characters, Milton and Joe.

2. Joe refers to Milton as his colleague. What does that show about how he views their relationship?

3. How did Milton manipulate Joe? In what ways did Joe manipulate Milton?

4. Milton meets eight girls who are a perfect match for him, yet he always feels like something is missing. Why is this?

5. What does Joe teach Milton about finding an ideal partner?

6. What did Milton eventually create?

7. The character, Milton Davidson, is described as being the person who "understands more about computers than anyone in the world . . ." Do you agree or disagree with this statement? Support your opinion with information from the text.

8. Why do you think Asimov chose to tell this story from the computer's point of view?

9. The story "True Love" was first published in 1977 and is an example of the science-fiction genre, which makes readers question the possibility of certain events presented in the story. This genre deals with topics such as new technological and scientific possibilities, space or time travel and extraterrestrial life. Science-fiction writers imagine situations that could possibly happen in the future. In what ways does this story fit the characteristics of the science-fiction genre? Provide examples from the story to support your ideas.

Beyond the Lines

10. Think about the information you would choose to share about yourself in order to find your ideal partner. Write a short paragraph that you could submit to an online dating service.

11. The story is told by the computer, Joe. Rewrite the important events in the story from Milton's point of view. Begin the story like this: My name is Milton. That is what my colleague, Joe, calls me.

12. Do you think that human beings in the 21st century are manipulated by machines? Are people today too dependent on technology? Write a paragraph to express your opinion on the subject.

Sherman Alexie, a Spokane/Coeur d'Alene Indian, was born in 1966 and grew up on the Spokane Indian Reservation in Wellpinit, Washington, in the United States. Born hydrocephalic, Alexie was not expected to survive, but surgery cured the problem, and he went on to beat the odds, learning to read by age three. *The Absolutely True Diary of a Part-Time Indian* is a novel based on the story of his decision to leave the reservation to go to high school, in order to get a better education. The novel won the 2007 National Book Award, and his other novels and poetry collections have won many awards as well. Alexie, who has performed stand-up comedy, is known for finding humour in even the most difficult of situations in his stories.

Before Reading

1. Draw a word web. In the middle circle, write the words Native American. Complete the word web with words associated with Native Americans.

2. What is a wake? Have you ever attended one?

3. What are some rituals associated with the death of someone?

4. Have you ever lost someone close to you? How did you pay tribute to that person or celebrate his or her life?

While Reading

5. Pay attention to words in the story related to Native Americans. Add new words to the word web you made in question 1 of the Before Reading section.

6. Point of view is the voice the author uses to tell the story. The author may use the first-person point of view (I) or the third-person point of view (he/she). What point of view does the author use in this story?

7. Describe the narrator of the story. What do you learn about the narrator through the language used to tell the story and the events described in the text?

From *The Absolutely True Diary of a Part-Time Indian*

by Sherman Alexie

W̲e held Grandmother's wake three days later. We knew that people would be coming in large
5 numbers. But we were stunned because almost two thousand Indians showed up that day to say good-bye.

And nobody gave me any crap.

I mean, I was still the kid who had betrayed the tribe. And that couldn't be forgiven. But I was also the kid who'd
10 lost his grandmother. And everybody knew that losing my grandmother was horrible. So they all waved the white flag that day and let me grieve in peace.

And after that, they stopped hassling me whenever they saw me on the rez. I mean, I still lived on the rez,
15 right? And I had to go get the mail and get milk from the trading post and just hang out, right? So I was still a part of the rez.

People had either ignored me or called me names or pushed me.

20 But they stopped after my grandmother died.

I guess they realized that I was in enough pain already. Or maybe they realized they'd been cruel jerks.

I wasn't suddenly popular, of course. But I wasn't a villain anymore.

25 No matter what else happened between my tribe and me, I would always love them for giving me peace on the day of my grandmother's funeral.

Even Rowdy just stood far away.

He would always be my best friend, no matter how
30 much he hated me.

We had to move the coffin out of the Spokane Tribal Longhouse and set it on the fifty-yard line of the football field.

We were lucky the weather was good.

35 Yep, about two thousand Indians (and a few white folks) sat and stood on the football field as we all said good-bye to the greatest Spokane Indian in history.

I knew that my grandmother would have loved that send-off.

40 It was crazy and fun and sad.

My sister wasn't able to come to the funeral. That was the worst part about it. She didn't have enough money to get back, I guess. That was sad. But she promised me she'd sing one hundred mourning songs that day.

45 We all have to find our own ways to say good-bye.

Tons of people told stories about my grandmother.

But there was one story that mattered most of all.

About ten hours into the wake, a white guy stood. He was a stranger. He looked vaguely familiar. I knew I'd seen
50 him before, but I couldn't think of where. We all wondered exactly who he was. But nobody knew. That wasn't surprising. My grandmother had met thousands of people.

The white guy was holding this big suitcase.

He held that thing tight to his chest as he talked.

55 "Hello," he said. "My name is Ted."

And then I remembered who he was. He was a rich and famous billionaire white dude. He was famous for being **filthy rich** and really weird.

My grandmother knew Billionaire Ted!

60 Wow.

We all were excited to hear this guy's story. And so what did he have to say?

We all **groaned**.

We'd expected this white guy to be original. But he was
65 yet another white guy who showed up on the rez because he loved Indian people SOOOOOOOO much.

Do you know how many white strangers show up on Indian reservations every year and start telling Indians how much they love them?

70 Thousands.

It's sickening.

And boring.

"Listen," Ted said. "I know you've heard that before. I know white people say that all the time. But I still need to
75 say it. I love Indians. I love your songs, your dances, and your souls. And I love your art. I collect Indian art."

Oh, God, he was a collector. Those guys made Indians feel
80 like insects pinned to a display board. I looked around the football field. Yep, all of my

From The Absolutely True Diary of a Part-Time Indian

cousins were squirming like beetles and butterflies with pins stuck in their hearts.

85   "I've collected Indian art for decades," Ted said. "I have old spears. Old arrowheads. I have old armor. I have blankets. And paintings. And sculptures. And baskets. And jewelry."

    Blah, blah, blah, blah.

90   "And I have old powwow dance outfits," he said.

    Now that made everybody sit up and pay attention.

    "About ten years ago, this Indian guy knocked on the door of my cabin in Montana."

    Cabin, my butt. Ted lived in a forty-room log mansion
95 just outside of Bozeman.

    "Well, I didn't know this stranger," Ted said. "But I always open my door to Indians."

    Oh, please.

    "And this particular Indian stranger was holding a very
100 beautiful powwow dance outfit, a woman's powwow dance outfit. It was the most beautiful thing I'd ever seen. It was all beaded blue and red and yellow with a thunderbird design. It must have weighed fifty pounds. And I couldn't

imagine the strength of the woman who could dance
105 beneath that magical **burden**."

Every woman in the world could dance that way.

"Well, this Indian stranger said he was in a desperate
situation. His wife was dying of cancer and he needed
money to pay for her medicine. I knew he was lying. I knew
110 he'd stolen the outfit. I could always smell a **thief**."

Smell yourself, Ted.

"And I knew I should call the police on this thief. I
knew I should take that **outfit** away and find the real
owner. But it was so beautiful, so perfect, that I gave the
115 Indian stranger a thousand dollars and sent him on his
way. And I kept the outfit."

Whoa, was Ted coming here to make a confession? And
why had he chosen my grandmother's funeral for his
confession?

120 "For years, I felt terrible. I'd look at that outfit hanging
on the wall of my Montana cabin."

Mansion, Ted it's a mansion. Go ahead; you can say it:
MANSION!

"And then I decided to do some research. I hired an
125 anthropologist, an expert, and he quickly pointed out that
the outfit was obviously of Interior Salish origin. And after
doing a little research, he discovered that the outfit was
Spokane Indian, to be specific. And then, a few years ago,
he visited your reservation undercover and learned that
130 this stolen outfit once belonged to a woman named
Grandmother Spirit."

We all gasped. This was a huge shock. I wondered if we
were all part of some crazy reality show called *When
Billionaires Pretend to be Human*. I looked around for the
135 cameras.

"Well, ever since I learned
who really owned this outfit,
I've been torn. I always wanted
to give it back. But I wanted to
140 keep it, too. I couldn't sleep
some nights because I was so
torn up by it."

Yep, even billionaires have DARK NIGHTS OF THE SOUL.

145   "And, well, I finally couldn't take it anymore. I packed up the outfit and headed for your reservation, here, to hand-deliver the outfit back to Grandmother Spirit. And I get here only to discover that she's passed on to the next world. It's just devastating."

150   We were all completely silent. This was the weirdest thing any of us had ever witnessed. And we're Indians, so trust me, we've seen some really weird stuff.

"But I have the outfit here," Ted said. He opened up his suitcase and pulled out the outfit and held it up. It was
155 fifty pounds, so he struggled with it. Anybody would have struggled with it.

"So if any of Grandmother Spirit's children are here, I'd love to return her outfit to them."

My mother stood and walked up to Ted.

160   "I'm Grandmother Spirit's only daughter," she said.

My mother's voice had gotten all formal. Indians are good at that. We'll be talking and laughing and carrying on like normal, and then, BOOM, we get all serious and sacred and start talking like some English royalty.

Sherman Alexie

165   "Dearest daughter," Ted said. "I hereby return your stolen goods, I hope you forgive me for returning it too late."

    "Well, there's nothing to forgive, Ted," my mother said. "Grandmother Spirit wasn't a powwow dancer."

170   Ted's mouth dropped open.

    "Excuse me," he said.

    "My mother loved going to powwows. But she never danced. She never owned a dance outfit. This couldn't be hers."

175   Ted didn't say anything. He couldn't say anything.

    "In fact, looking at the beads and design, this doesn't look Spokane at all. I don't recognize the work. Does anybody here recognize the **beadwork**?"

    "No," everybody said.

180   "It looks more Sioux to me," my mother said. "Maybe Oglala. Maybe. I'm not an expert. Your anthropologist wasn't much of an expert, either. He got this *way* wrong."

    We all just sat there in silence as Ted **mulled** that **over**.

185   Then he packed his outfit back into the suitcase, hurried over to his waiting car, and sped away.

    For about two minutes, we all sat quiet. Who knew what to say? And then my mother started laughing.

    And that set us all off.

190   Two thousand Indians laughed at the same time.

    We kept laughing.

    It was the most glorious noise I'd ever heard.

    And I realized that, sure, Indians were drunk and sad and displaced and crazy and mean, but, dang, we knew

195 how to laugh.

    When it comes to death, we know that laughter and tears are pretty much the same thing.

    And so, laughing and crying, we said good-bye to my

200 grandmother. And when we said good-bye to one grandmother, we said good-bye to all of them.

    Each funeral was a funeral for all of us.

VOCABULARY

beadwork: decoration made with beads

mulled over: thought about carefully

From *The Absolutely True Diary of a Part-Time Indian*

205   We lived and died together.
       All of us laughed when they lowered my grandmother
into the ground.
       And all of us laughed when they covered her with dirt.
       And all of us laughed as we walked and drove and rode
210 our way back to our lonely, lonely houses.

Sherman Alexie

After Reading

1. Sherman Alexie is known for his humorous style of writing. Authors use various techniques to create humour in their stories. Some of these techniques are listed below. Find an example of each one in the story.

Technique	
Characterization (character's speech, thoughts and actions)	
Illustrations/photos	
Events in the story	
Exaggeration/hyperbole	
Understatement	
Sarcasm	

2. What impact does Alexie's use of humour have on the description of the funeral?

3. Why does the narrator think his grandmother would like the funeral?

4. Who is the "white guy" that attends the funeral and what does he want? What reaction does his presence cause among the others attending the funeral?

5. What part of the "white guy's" story catches the audience's attention? Why do you think this is?

6. What finally happens in the episode with Ted? What is ironic about how the situation ends?

7. What do you think about the author's use of illustrations within the text? Which of the illustrations do you prefer? Explain your answer.

Beyond the Lines

8. This text is an excerpt from the novel *The Absolutely True Diary of a Part-Time Indian*. Based on the title and the information provided in the excerpt you read, do you think you would like to read the novel? Explain your answer.

9. The narrator in the story, like the author Sherman Alexie, betrays his tribe by leaving to go to school with the white people. Do you think he did the right thing? Do you think getting an education is worth being alienated from your heritage or cultural roots?

Alice Munro, born in Wingham, Ontario, in 1931, is considered to be one of the world's finest writers of fiction. A three-time Governor General's Award Winner, she writes short stories that are known for their small-town settings and their characters' struggles with love and work. One of 16 collections of short stories, her collection *The View from Castle Rock,* where "Hired Girl" appears, is an example of her use of historical and autobiographical details in her stories.

Before Reading

1. What summer jobs have you held in the past? What type of job would you most like to have?

2. What do you think life was like in small towns across Canada in the mid 20th century? Think about male and female roles as well as the difference in social classes. Do you think life was much different from life today?

While Reading

3. The author, Alice Munro, is known for writing stories about characters in conflict that take place in small towns. Find information in the story to support each of the following elements of the author's style.

Small-town setting	
Character's struggle with love or work	
Historical details	
Autobiographical details	

4. Describe the setting of the story. Make a list of words and phrases that give you clues as to where and when the story takes place.

5. Pay attention to information about the narrator of the story. What do you learn about her?

From "Hired Girl"

by Alice Munro

Mrs. Montjoy was showing me how to put the pots and pans away. I had put some of them in the wrong places.

Above all things, she said, she hated a higgledy-
5 piggledy cupboard.

"You waste more time," she said. "You waste more time looking for something because it wasn't where it was last time."

"That's the way it was with our hired girls at home," I
10 said. "The first few days they were there they were always putting things away where we couldn't find them.

"We called our maids hired girls," I added. "That was what we called them, at home."

"Did you?" she said. A moment of silence passed. "And
15 the colander on that hook there."

Why did I have to say what I had said? Why was it necessary to mention that we had hired girls at home?

Anybody could see why. To put myself somewhere near her level. As if that was possible. As if anything I had to say
20 about myself or the house I came from could interest or impress her.

It was true, though, about the hired girls. In my early life there was a procession of them. There was Olive, a soft drowsy girl who didn't like me because I called her Olive Oyl. Even after I was made to apologize she didn't like me. Maybe she didn't like any of us much because she was a Bible Christian, which made her mistrustful and reserved. She used to sing as she washed the dishes and I dried. *There is a Balm in Gilead* . . . If I tried to sing with her she stopped.

Then came Jeanie, whom I liked, because she was pretty and she did my hair up in pin curls at night when she did her own. She kept a list of the boys she went out with and made peculiar signs after their names: x x o o * *. She did not last long.

Neither did Dorothy, who hung the clothes on the line in an eccentric way—pinned up by the collar, or by one sleeve or one leg—and swept the dirt into a corner and propped the broom up to hide it.

And when I was around ten years old hired girls became a thing of the past. I don't know if it was because we became poorer or because I was considered old enough to be a steady help. Both things were true.

Now I was seventeen and able to be hired out myself, though only as summer help because I had one more year to go at high school. My sister was twelve, so she could take over at home.

Mrs. Montjoy had picked me up at the railway station in Pointe au Baril, and transported me in an outboard-motor boat to the island. It was the woman in the Pointe au Baril store who had recommended me for the job. She was an old friend of my mother's—they had taught school together. Mrs. Montjoy had asked her if she knew of a country girl, used to doing housework, who would be available for the summer, and the woman had thought that it would be the very thing for me. I thought so too—I was **eager** to see more of the world.

Mrs. Montjoy wore khaki shorts and a tucked-in shirt. Her short, sun-bleached hair was pushed behind her ears. She leapt aboard the boat like a boy and gave a fierce tug to the motor, and we were flung out on the choppy evening waters of Georgian Bay. For thirty or forty minutes we dodged around rocky and wooded islands with their lone cottages and boats bobbing beside the docks. Pine trees jutted out at odd angles, just as they do in the paintings.

I held on to the sides of the boat and **shivered** in my **flimsy** dress.

"Feeling a tad sick?" said Mrs. Montjoy, with the briefest possible smile. It was like the signal for a smile, when the occasion did not warrant the real thing. She had large white teeth in a long tanned face, and her natural expression seemed to be one of impatience barely **held in check**. She probably knew that what I was feeling was fear, not sickness, and she threw out this question so that I—and she—need not be embarrassed.

Here was a difference, already, from the world I was used to. In that world, fear was commonplace, at least for females. You could be afraid of snakes, thunderstorms, deep

water, heights, the dark, the bull, and the lonely road through the swamp, and nobody thought any the worse of
85 you. In Mrs. Montjoy's world, however, fear was shameful and always something to be conquered.

The island that was our destination had a name—Nausicaa. The name was written on a board at the end of the dock. I said it aloud, trying to show that I was at ease
90 and quietly appreciative, and Mrs. Montjoy said with slight surprise, "Oh, yes. That was the name it already had when Daddy bought it. It's for some character in Shakespeare."

I opened up my mouth to say no, no, not Shakespeare, and to tell her that Nausicaa was the girl on the beach,
95 playing ball with her friends, surprised by Ulysses when he woke up from his nap. I had learned by this time that most of the people I lived amongst did not welcome this kind of information, and I would probably have kept quiet even if the teacher had asked us in school, but I believed
100 that people out in the world—the real world—would be different. Just in time I recognized the **briskness** of Mrs. Montjoy's tone when she said "some character in Shakespeare"—the suggestion that Nausicaa, and

Shakespeare, as well as any observations of mine, were
105 things she could reasonably do without.

The dress I was wearing for my arrival was one I had
made myself, out of pink and white striped cotton. The
material had been cheap, the reason being that it was not
really meant for a dress but for a blouse or a nightgown,
110 and the style I had chosen—the full-skirted, tight-waisted
style of those days—was a mistake. When I walked, the
cloth bunched up between my legs, and I kept having to
yank it loose. Today was the first day the dress had been
worn, and I still thought that the trouble might be
115 temporary—with a firm enough yank the material might
be made to hang properly. But I found when I took off my
belt that the day's heat and my hot ride on the train had
created a worse problem. The belt was wide and elasticized,
and of a burgundy color, which had run. The waistline of
120 the dress was circled with strawberry dye.

I made this discovery when I was getting undressed in
the loft of the boathouse, which I was to share with Mrs.
Montjoy's ten-year-old daughter, Mary Anne.

"What happened to your dress?" Mary Anne said. "Do
125 you sweat a lot? That's too bad."

I said that it was an old dress anyway and that I hadn't
wanted to wear anything good on the train.

Mary Anne was fair-haired and **freckled**, with a long
face like her mother's. But she didn't have her mother's
130 look of quick judgments **marshalled** at the surface, ready
to leap out at you. Her expression was benign and serious,
and she wore heavy glasses even when sitting up in bed.
She was to tell me soon that she
had had an operation to get her
135 eyes straightened, but even so
her eyesight was poor.

"I've got Daddy's eyes," she
said. "I'm intelligent like him
too so it's too bad I'm not a boy."
140 Another difference. Where I
came from, it was generally
held to be more suspect for
boys to be smart than for girls

VOCABULARY

briskness: haste;
sharpness

freckled: covered with
small, brownish spots
on the skin

marshalled: arranged
and ordered

yank: pull abruptly

to be, though not particularly advantageous for one or the
145 other. Girls could go on to be teachers, and that was all right—though quite often they became old maids—but for boys to continue with school usually meant they were **sissies**.

All night long you could hear the water slapping
150 against the boards of the boathouse. Morning came early. I wondered whether I was far enough north of home for the sun to actually be rising sooner. I got up and looked out. Through the front window, I saw the silky water, dark underneath but flashing back from its surface the light of
155 the sky. The rocky shores of this little cove, the **moored** sailboats, the open channel beyond, the mound of another island or two, shores and channels beyond that. I thought that I would never, on my own, be able to find my way back to the mainland.

160 I did not yet understand that maids didn't have to find their way anywhere. They stayed put, where the work was. It was the people who made the work who could come and go.

VOCABULARY

moored: secured to a dock or anchor

sissy: an effeminate boy or man

After Reading

1. Who is Mrs. Montjoy and what type of person is she?

2. Why does the narrator mention the hired girls she and her family had at home?

3. Name and provide one piece of information about the three hired girls who worked for the narrator's family when she was young.

4. Why did the narrator's family stop hiring girls?

5. How did the narrator get the job working for Mrs. Montjoy?

6. How does the narrator feel about her summer job at first?

7. Use a graphic organizer to compare and contrast the two worlds described in the story—where the narrator comes from and the new society in which she arrives.

8. Where were Mrs. Montjoy and the narrator travelling to?

9. Why does the narrator choose not to correct Mrs. Montjoy when she explains the origins of the island's name?

10. Do you think the narrator is an educated girl? Find information in the story to support your answer.

11. How is Mary Anne similar to and different from her mother?

12. According to this story, what is the destiny of a maid?

Beyond the Lines

13. What message do you think the author is trying to share with her readers? What lesson can you learn from this story?

14. Describe an experience you or someone you know had that is similar to something experienced by one of the characters in the story.

15. Have attitudes toward education in our society today changed from the attitudes of the society described in this story? In what ways?

Teolinda Gersão was born in Coimbra, Portugal, in 1940. Before beginning her writing career, she taught Portuguese, German and comparative literature at several European universities. Her stories and novels often deal with the problems of identity and time, where fantasy and the subconscious meet up with everyday reality. Her work in her native language has received several literary awards, and it has been translated into several other languages, including English, German and French.

Before Reading

1. Read the title of the story. What do you think it will be about?

2. Read the list of words below. Using the prediction you made in question 1 as your theme, write a short paragraph using as many of the words as you can, underlining the words you used in your paragraph.

shiver	sniff	heartbeat	devour
desire	prowl	flames	gnaw
fire	nail	satisfaction	tempestuous
unique	raw	nimble	blood

3. Describe a situation in which you felt like you had to act or behave in a way that did not represent who you really are. How did it make you feel?

While Reading

4. Authors use vivid and descriptive language to create imagery in stories. Imagery appeals to your senses and helps you to fully experience the events in the story. While you read, look for examples of imagery and write down key words and phrases in a chart like the one shown below.

Sight	Sound	Taste	Touch	Smell

"The Red Fox Fur Coat"

by Teolinda Gersão

Translated from the Portuguese
by Margaret Jull Costa

O n her way home one day, a humble bank clerk
happened to see a red fox fur coat in a furrier's shop
window. She stopped outside and felt a shiver of pleasure
and desire run through her. For this was the coat she had
5 always wanted. There wasn't another one like it, she
thought, running her eyes over the other coats hanging
from the metal rack or delicately draped over a brocade
sofa. It was rare, unique; she had never seen such a color,
golden, with a coppery sheen, and so bright it looked as if
10 it were on fire. The shop was closed at the time, as she
discovered when, giving in to the impulse to enter, she
pushed at the door. She would come back tomorrow, as
early as possible, on her lunch break, or during the
morning; yes, she would find a pretext to slip out during
15 the morning. That night she slept little and awoke feeling
troubled and slightly feverish. She counted the minutes
until the shop would open; her eyes wandered from the
clock on the wall to her wristwatch and back, while she
dealt with various customers. As soon as she could, she
20 found an excuse to pop out and run to the shop, trembling
to think that the coat might have been sold. It had not, she

learned, been sold; she felt her breath return, her heartbeat ease, felt the blood drain from her face and resume its measured flow.

25 "It could have been made for you," said the saleswoman when the bank clerk put the coat on and looked at herself in the mirror. "It fits perfectly on the shoulders and at the waist, and the length is just right," she said, "and it really suits your skin tone. Not that I'm trying
30 to pressure you into buying it," she added hurriedly, "obviously you're free to choose anything you like, but if you don't mind my saying so, the coat really does look as if it had been made for you. Just for you," she said again, with the hint of a smile.

35 "How much is it?" the bank clerk asked, half turning round thus setting the hem of the coat swinging—because she found it hard to take her eyes off her own image in the mirror.

She **recoiled**, stunned, when she heard the reply. It
40 cost far more than she had thought, five times more than she could possibly afford.

"But we can spread out the payment if you like," said the saleswoman kindly.

She could always sacrifice her holidays, the bank clerk
45 thought. Or divert some of the money intended for a car loan. She could use less heating, eat smaller meals. It would do her good, really, because she was beginning to put on a bit of weight.

"All right," she said, doing rapid calculations in her
50 head. "I'll give you a deposit and start paying next week. But it's definitely mine now, isn't it?"

"Absolutely," said the saleswoman, attaching a "Sold" label to the coat. "You can take it away with you when you've paid the third installment."

55 She started visiting the shop at night, when it was closed and no one would see her, in order to gaze at the coat through the window, and each time it brought her more joy, each time it was brighter, more **fiery**, like red flames that did not burn, but were soft on her body, like
60 a thick, ample, enfolding skin that moved when she moved . . .

It would be admired, as would she, people would turn to stare after her, but it was not this that provoked a secret smile; rather, she realized, it was an inner satisfaction, an

65 obscure certainty, a sense of being in harmony with herself, that spilled over in all kinds of small ways. It was as if the rhythm of her breathing had changed, had grown calmer and deeper. She realized too, perhaps because she no longer felt tired, that she moved more quickly, that she could walk

70 effortlessly now, at twice her usual speed. Her legs were agile, her feet **nimble**. Everything about her was lighter, quicker; her back, shoulders, and limbs all moved more easily.

It must be all the keep-fit I've been doing, she thought,

75 because for some reason she had started taking regular exercise. For a few months now she had been spending two hours a week running at the track. But what she liked most was to go running in the forest, on the outskirts of the city, feeling the sand crunch beneath her feet, learning to place

80 her feet on the ground in a different way—in direct, perfect, intimate contact with the earth. She was intensely aware of her body; she was more alive now, more alert. All her senses were **keener** too, she could hear, even from some distance away, **infinitesimal** sounds which, before,

85 would have gone unnoticed: a lizard **scurrying** through the leaves, an invisible mouse making a twig crack, an acorn falling, a bird landing on a bush; she could sense atmospheric changes long before they happened: the wind turning, a rise in humidity, an increase in air pressure that

90 would culminate in rain.

And another aspect of all the things to which she had now become sensitized was the discovery of smells, a whole

95 world of smells; she could find paths and trails purely by smell; it was strange how she had never before noticed that everything has a smell: the earth, the

100 bark of trees, plants, leaves, and that every animal can be

VOCABULARY

fiery: like fire

infinitesimal: extremely small

keener: more sensitive

nimble: agile

recoiled: moved back in surprise or horror

scurrying: moving quickly

distinguished by its own peculiar smell, a whole spectrum of smells that came to her on waves through the air, and which she could draw together or separate out, sniffing the
105 wind, imperceptibly lifting her head.

She suddenly became very interested in animals and found herself leafing through encyclopedias, looking at the pictures—the **hedgehog's** pale, soft, tender underbelly; the swift hare, of uncertain hue, leaping; she pored over the
110 bodies of birds, fascinated, pondering the softness of the flesh behind their feathers; and a single word kept bobbing insistently about in her mind: predator.

She seemed to be hungrier too, she thought, as she put away her books and went into the kitchen, and this
115 negative aspect to all the physical exercise displeased her greatly. She tried to find a way to avoid putting on weight and prowled, dissatisfied, past patisseries, never finding what she was looking for, because the smell of coffee was repellent to her and made her feel nauseous. No, she was
120 hungry for other things, although she didn't quite know what, fruit perhaps; this might be an opportunity to lose a little weight. She bought a vast quantity of grapes and

apples and ate them all in one day, but still she felt hungry, a hidden hunger that **gnawed** at her from inside and never stopped.

She was cheered by an unexpected invitation to a party, welcoming any diversion that would make her forget that absurd hunger. She reveled in getting dressed up and in painting her lips and nails scarlet. Her nails, she noticed, were very long, and even her hands seemed more sensitive, more elongated. Anyone she touched at the party that night would remain eternally in her power, she thought, smiling at herself in the mirror—a feline smile, it seemed to her. She narrowed her eyes and widened the smile, letting it spread over her face, which took on a pleasingly triangular shape that she further emphasized with make-up.

In the middle of the party, she noticed someone slicing up some meat, cooked very rare—roast beef, she thought, although these words had suddenly ceased to have any meaning. She reached out her hand and devoured a whole slice. Ah, she thought, the taste of almost raw meat, the action of sinking her teeth into it, of making the blood spurt, the taste of blood on her tongue, in her mouth, the innocence of devouring the whole slice, and she took another slice, already sensing that using her hand was now a pointless waste of time, that she should just pick it up directly with her mouth.

She burst out laughing and began to dance, waving her bloodstained hands in the air, feeling her own blood rise, as if some tempestuous inner force had been **unleashed**, a malign force that she could transmit to others, a plague or a curse, but this idea was nevertheless sweet, quiet, almost joyful, she felt, as she swayed, slightly drunk, listening to the echo of her own laughter.

She would spend the night obeying all these newly released forces and, in the morning, she would go and fetch the coat, because the day had come when it would be hers; it was part of her; she would know it even with her eyes closed, by touch

VOCABULARY

gnawed: ate

hedgehog: a small animal with spikes on its back and sides

unleashed: set loose

alone, the soft, thick **pelt** <u>burning her skin</u>, **cleaving** to her, until she could no longer tell skin from skin . . .

"It could have been made for you," the saleswoman said again, as she removed it from the coat hanger.

The coat cleaving to her, until she could no longer tell skin from skin, as she could see in the mirror, as she turned the collar up around her head, her face disfigured, suddenly thinner, made up to look longer, her eyes narrow, restless, burning . . .

"Goodbye, then, and thanks," she said, rushing out of the shop, afraid that time was getting short and that people would stop in alarm to stare at her, because suddenly the impulse to go down on all fours and simply run was too strong, reincarnating her body, rediscovering her animal body; and as she fled, as she left the city behind her and simply fled, it took an almost superhuman effort to get into her car and drive to the edge of the forest, keeping tight control of her body, keeping tight control of her tremulous body for just one more minute, before that slam of the door, that first genuine leap on feet free at last, shaking her back and her tail, <u>sniffing</u> the air, the ground, the wind, and, with a howl of pleasure and joy, plunging off into the depths of the forest.

VOCABULARY

cleaving: clinging to very closely
pelt: animal skin

After Reading

1. What is the woman's job?

2. Describe the coat that the woman sees in the shop window.

3. The woman immediately becomes obsessed with the fur coat and thinks about it day and night. Why do you think this is?

4. What is the woman prepared to sacrifice in order to buy the fur coat?

5. What did the woman start to do at night?

6. Is the idea of being admired by other people important to the woman? Find a sentence in the text to support your answer.

7. What physical changes does the woman undergo throughout the story?

8. What reason does the woman give for her increased energy and agility?

9. As the story continues, the main character's animal instincts become progressively stronger. Trace the changes that the main character experiences throughout the story.

10. How does the woman attempt to satisfy her insatiable hunger?

11. What does the woman finally achieve at the end of the story?

12. Because of the high price of the fur coat, the woman cannot afford to pay for it all at once and cannot take it home right away. What impact does this have on the story? How would things have been different if she had taken the coat home right away?

13. Look at the chart you completed in question 4 of the While Reading section. What senses does the author evoke most often?

14. How does the use of imagery contribute to your understanding of the story? Select your favorite passage from the text containing strong imagery and explain why you chose it.

Beyond the Lines

15. What do you think the woman's transformation represents?

16. Write a paragraph sharing your reaction to this story. Explain what you liked or disliked and support your answer with information from the text.

Sources

Texts

p. 2: "Powder," from *Night in Question* by Tobias Wolff, © 1996 by Tobias Wolff. Used by permission of Alfred A. Knopf, a division of Random House, Inc.

p. 10: "The Lottery Ticket," from *The Wife, and Other Stories* by Anton Chekhov, translated by Constance Garnett. Public domain.

p. 18: Reprinted with permission of Scribner, a Division of Simon & Schuster, Inc., from *The Girl Who Loved Tom Gordon* by Stephen King. © 1999 by Stephen King. All rights reserved.

p. 28: "Tomorrow's Bird" from *Lamentations of the Father* by Ian Frazier. © 2008 by Ian Frazier. Reprinted by permission of Farrar, Straus and Giroux, LLC.

p. 36: Excerpted from *The Blue Helmet* by William Bell. © 2006 William Bell. Reprinted by permission of Doubleday Canada.

p. 46: "A Conversation with My Father" from *Enormous Changes at the Last Minute* by Grace Paley. © 1971, 1974 by Grace Paley. Reprinted by permission of Farrar, Straus and Giroux, LLC.

p. 56: "The Diamond Necklace," from *Original Short Stories*, Vol. IV, by Guy de Maupassant, translated by Albert McMaster, A. E. Henderson and Louise Charlotte Garstin Quesada. Public domain.

p. 68: "The Unsanded Balloon." © 2003 Carrie Haber. Reprinted with the author's permission.

p. 76: "No Justice, No Peace," "Advice from a Smart Mouth," and "The Beast Prowls" from *Speak* by Laurie Halse Anderson. © 1999 by Laurie Halse Anderson. Reprinted by permission of Farrar, Straus and Giroux, LLC.

p. 84: "All the Years of Her Life" from *Morley Callaghan's Stories* by Morley Callaghan. Reprinted by permission of the author's son, Barry Callaghan.

p. 94: Chapter originally entitled "The Wildcat" from *A Thief in the House of Memory* by Tim Wynne-Jones. © 2004 by Tim Wynne-Jones. Reprinted by permission of Farrar, Straus and Giroux, LLC.

p. 102: Excerpted from "The Boarded Window" from *The Collected Works of Ambrose Bierce*, Vol. II, by Ambrose Bierce. Public domain.

p. 110: "A Golden Wedding," from *Lucy Maud Montgomery Short Stories, 1909 to 1922* by L. M. Montgomery. Public domain.

p. 120: Short story, "Celia Behind Me," in *The Elizabeth Stories*, by Isabel Huggan (Oberon Press, ISBN 978 0 88750 520 1). Reprinted with the author's permission.

p. 132: "True Love," © 1977 by American Airlines, Inc., from *The Complete Robot* by Isaac Asimov. Used by permission of Doubleday, a division of Random House, Inc.

p. 140: From *The Absolutely True Diary of a Part-Time Indian* by Sherman Alexie. © 2007 by Sherman Alexie. Illustrations © 2007 by Ellen Forney. By permission of Little, Brown & Company.

p. 150: Excerpt from short story "Hired Girl," pp. 227-231, from *The View from Castle Rock* by Alice Munro © 2006. Published by McClelland & Stewart Ltd. Used with permission of the publisher.

p. 158: "The Red Fox Fur Coat" by Teolinda Gersão, translated from the Portuguese by Margaret Jull Costa. Reprinted with the author's permission.

Photos

p. 2: Getty Images • **p. 3:** Vladimir Zivkovic/Shutterstock • **p. 5:** Karol Kozlowski/Shutterstock • **p. 6:** Yurlov Andrey/Shutterstock • **p. 8:** William Walsh/iStockphoto • **p. 10:** akg-images • **p. 11:** E. Sweet/Shutterstock • **p. 14:** Sean Gladwell/Shutterstock • **p. 18:** courtesy StephenKing.com • **p. 19:** Vasiliy Koval/Shutterstock • **p. 21:** MitarArt/Shutterstock • **p. 24:** Edwin Verin/Shutterstock • **p. 28:** Sigrid Estrada • **p. 29:** Eric Isselée/Shutterstock • **p. 31:** Feliks/Shutterstock • **p. 32:** Orkhan Aslanov/Shutterstock • **p. 36:** courtesy William Bell • **p. 37:** Alexander Efimov/Shutterstock • **p. 38:** Wallenrock/Shutterstock • **p. 42:** Rob Byron/Shutterstock • **p. 46:** gentl & hyers/edge • **p. 47:** baki/Shutterstock • **p. 49:** Falko Matte/Shutterstock • **p. 50:** Janaka/Shutterstock • **p. 52:** Marcin Moryc/Shutterstock • **p. 56:** HenryGuttmann/HultonArchive/Getty Images • **p. 57:** Angelina M. Scully/Shutterstock • **p. 60:** Transition/Shutterstock • **p. 64:** Nikuwka/Shutterstock • **p. 68:** courtesy Carrie Haber • **p. 69:** bluecrayola/Shutterstock • **p. 70:** 5464316719/Shutterstock • **p. 72:** Wendy Sue Gilman/Shutterstock • **p. 76:** Joyce Tenneson • **p. 77:** Gremlin/iStockphoto • **p. 79:** Hal Bergman/iStockphoto • **p. 81:** KUCO/Shutterstock • **p. 84:** Nigel Dickson • **p. 85:** Denis and Yulia Pogostins/Shutterstock • **p. 88:** Graeme Dawes/Shutterstock • **p. 91:** Eduardo Jose Bernardino/iStockphoto • **p. 94:** courtesy Tim Wynne-Jones • **p. 95:** Joe Mercier/Shutterstock • **p. 96:** Ales Nowak/Shutterstock • **p. 98:** Andrejs Pidjass/Shutterstock • **p. 102:** Ambrose Bierce 1866, Special Collections, University of Virginia Library • **p. 103:** Nicolas McComber/Shutterstock • **p. 104** Manuel Velasco/iStockphoto • **p. 107:** Kristalls/Shutterstock • **p. 110:** National Archives/ Canadian Press • **p. 111:** Ilin Sergey/Shutterstock • **p. 113:** Ian Shaw/Getty Images • **p. 115:** Ami Beyer/Shutterstock • **p. 116:** Elena Elisseeva/Shutterstock • **p. 117:** Michael Drager/Shutterstock • **p. 120:** Glenn Lowson • **p. 121:** John Kroetch/Shutterstock • **p. 124:** Jennie Book/Shutterstock • **p. 128:** kdow/iStockphoto • **p. 132:** © Yousuf Karsh • **p. 133:** Feng Yu/Shutterstock • **p. 135:** © Colin Anderson/Blend Images/Corbis • **p. 136:** bluecrayola/Shutterstock • **p. 137:** Ioana Drutu/Shutterstock • **p. 140:** © Rob Casey/Photo Shelter • **p. 141:** Jason Cheever/Shutterstock • **pp. 142, 144, 146:** Illustrations copyright 2007 by Ellen Forney. By permission of Little, Brown & Company. • **p. 150:** Derek Shapton • **p. 151:** Madeleine Openshaw/Shutterstock • **p. 152:** Stefanie Mohr Photography/Shutterstock • **p. 154:** Joshua Rainey Photography/Shutterstock • **p. 158:** courtesy Teolinda Gersão • **p. 159:** Terekhov Igor/Shutterstock • **p. 162:** Jason Boeselager/iStockphoto • **p. 164:** Helen E. Grose/Shutterstock